THE CELTIC DRAGON MYTH

BY J. F. CAMPBELL

Collector of "The West Highland Tales"

WITH THE

GESTE OF FRAOCH AND THE DRAGON

TRANSLATED WITH INTRODUCTION

BY GEORGE HENDERSON

PH.D. (Vienna); B.LITT. (Oxon.); M.A. (Edin.)

Lecturer in Celtic Languages and Literature, University of Glasgow

1911

This book has been published by:

Contact: sales@ezreads.net

URL: http://www.ezreads.net

Publishing Date: 2009

ISBN# 978-1-61534-000-2

Striving to be a leader in digital publishing. All of our books have been digitalized and reformatted to be EZ to Read and available in Paperback, two types of Hardcover and several eBook formats. See our website for a wide range of subjects including most religions, philosophy, historical, classical fiction, freemasonry, esoteric and ancient texts.

Please note that we do not correct out-of-date facts or grammar-type errors that were in the original book. We do our best to retain the original composition of the text, the way the author intended it.

CONTENTS

" If the king's daughter is not here to-morrow at this same hour the realm shall be ravaged by me," said the dragon. (*See* p. 61.)

INTRODUCTION

BETWEEN the years 1870 and 1884 the late Mr J. F. Campbell of Islay was repeatedly attracted by a series of legends current in the Highlands and Isles, which made special appeal to him as a storyologist. After reading a dozen versions of the stories, he found that no single title fitted so well as that of the *Dragon Myth*. "It treats of water, egg, mermaid, sea-dragon, tree, beasts, birds, fish, metals, weapons, and men mysteriously produced from sea-gifts. All versions agree in these respects; they are all water myths, and relate to the slaying of water monsters."

As early indeed as 1862, while fresh from work, he had taken incidents from three versions and compared them with versions in other languages. Several journeys in the Highlands followed, as also in Japan, China, and Ceylon. While in the East, it was part of his pastimes to make sketches of the Dragons of the Orient, his mind being all the while full of the legends of the West. He regarded this as one of the most important of myths, and the most difficult to deal with. It is the State Myth of England, Russia, and Japan. He found it in the "Rig Veda," and he concluded generally that it is Eur-Aryan in the widest sense.

Of his own work he expressly says that it is free translation. "I take the story from the Gaelic and tell it in my own words generally where the scribe's language is prosy. But when passages occur which seem worth preservation—bits of recitation and quaint phrases—I have translated carefully. This is work honestly done while my head was full of the subject. I think that it might interest a large number of readers... ." The manuscript is among the Campbell of Islay Collection in the Advocates' Library, Edinburgh, to the Curators of which I am beholden for their courtesy, of which I now make public acknowledgment, in enabling me to complete at

Glasgow University Library the transcription which I had begun many years ago.

For him the subject had two distinct aspects: first, the story is amusing for children; secondly, it has a scientific interest for a large and growing number of scholars. He had heard in London Mr Ralston give his lectures upon Russian stories, and found that the children in the audience were much amused. But amongst the audience were also Thomas Carlyle, Professor Owen, Sir R. Murchison, Reeve, Lady Ashburton, Miss Dempster of Skibo, and a number of learned people who wanted to know "the philosophy of the subject." For Mr Campbell thought there was a great deal of philosophy in it, and he states: "I want readers, wise and foolish, to be equally well treated. The foolish may read the story, the wise may read both story and notes."

He had read parallel stories in Swedish, German, French, Italian, English, and had heard outlines of Russian versions which seemed to him more mythical and nearer the original shape. He even found a part of the story in a book of Swahili tales told at Zanzibar.

"Theoretically," he remarks in 1876, this looks like serpent worship, and the defeat of serpent worship by some mythical personage. Many of the incidents which are not in Gaelic, but are in Swedish, can be traced, and are explained in the Russian version, e.g., a well is a serpent, an apple tree is another serpent, a cushion in á meadow is a third serpent transformed. Three brothers are concerned in Russian. In Swedish the serpent-slaying heroes are born of maidens who in one instance drink of a well, and in the other eat an apple. Three brothers are concerned in the adventures in Gaelic in one case, and incidents enough for three are in the several versions; if they were combined, Gaelic Swedish and Russian together would make something like a fragment of mythology, but the Gaelic versions give the largest quantity of materials."

The incidents, which number about 440, or deducting what are but variants, about 200, were put together from the following Gaelic versions or stories (of which some specimens are given in this book) collected between January 1856 and January 1861. They are:—

1. *Sea-Maiden*, No. IV., Popular Tales of the West Highlands, p. 72. Hector Urquhart and John Mackenzie, Inveraray.

2. *The Three Roads*. Hector Maclean and B. Macaskill, Berneray. MS.

3. *The Fisher's Son and The Daughter of the King of the Golden Castle*. John Dewar; J. MacNair, Clachaig, Cowal. MS.

4. *The Five-headed Giant*. B. Macaskill, Berneray; and Hector Maclean. MS.

5. *The Smith's Son*. Same sources. MS.

6. *The Fisher*. Hector Maclean and Alexander MacNeil, Ceanntangaval, Barra. MS.

7. *The Gray Lad*. Hector Maclean and John Smith, Polchar, S. Uist. MS.

8. *The Second Son of the King of Ireland and The Daughter of the King of France*. J. Dewar; J. MacNair, Clachaig, Cowal. MS.

9. *The Sea Maiden*. MS. notes by J. F. C., and John MacPhie, vol. i., Popular Tales. Interleaved copy, second recitation.

10. *The Sea Maiden*. Pp. 328, 346 of English Collection by J. F. C. Notes and MSS.

11. *Notes* from an Irish blind fiddler on the Loch Goil Head steamer. Interleaved copy. Popular Tales, vol i., p. 71.

Then came further Gaelic versions noted in 1870 and later:—

12. *Notes* in Journal, Aug. 17, 1870, pp. 1-10, from Lachlan MacNeill,[1] 5 Maxwellton Street, Paisley.

13. Aug. 22, 1870. "John Mackenzie, fisherman, can repeat the story as printed from his telling in my book. Kenmore, Inveraray."

---

[1] The reciter of *Leigheas Cois' O Céin*, published by me in the *Transactions of the Gaelic Society of Inverness*.

14. *Iain Beag Mac An Iasgair* (Little John the Fisher's Son); p. 42 of J. F. C.'s Journal for Sept. 1, 1870. From Malcolm MacDonald, fisherman, Benmore Cottage, Mull.

15. *Fionn Mac A Bhradain agus Donnchadh mac a' Bhradain.* From — Maclean, fisherman, Bunessan, Ross of Mull.

It will be seen that the legends ranged over a wide Highland area; were thoroughly popular, and of the people. In Ireland there are references to the Dragon story also in Hyde's *Sgeulaidhe*, and one may compare Synge's *The Aran Isles* (pp. 40, 46, 24, 55). Parallel tales of contests with water-monsters are world-wide, and the story of St George and the Dragon, as told in Palestine, is very similar to that current in the Highlands. At Beyrût is shown the very well into which he cast the slain monster, and the place where the saint washed his hands thereafter. The story is:—

"There was once a great city that depended for its water-supply upon a fountain without the walls. A great dragon, possessed and moved by Satan himself, took possession of the fountain and refused to allow water to be taken unless, whenever people came to the spring, a youth or maiden was given to him to devour. The people tried again and again to destroy the monster, but though the flower of the city cheerfully went forth against it, its breath was so pestilential that they used to drop down dead before they came within bowshot.

The terrorised inhabitants were thus obliged to sacrifice their offspring, or die of thirst; till at last all the youths of the place had perished except the king's daughter. So great was the distress of their subjects for want of water that the heart-broken parents could no longer withhold her, and amid the tears of the populace she went out towards the spring where the dragon lay awaiting her. But just as the noisome monster was going to leap on her, Mar Jiryis appeared, in golden panoply upon a fine white steed, and spear in hand. Riding full tilt at the dragon, he struck it fair between the eyes and laid it dead. The king, out of gratitude for this unlooked-for succour, gave Mar Jiryis his daughter and half of his kingdom."[2]

In the folk-lore of China there is a popular legend that the Chien Tang River was once infested by a great *kiau* or sea-serpent, and in 1129 A.D. a district graduate is said to have heroically thrown himself into the flood to encounter and destroy the monster. Formerly two dragons were supposed by the Chinese to have been in a narrow passage near Chinaye: they were very furious, and upset boats. According to the Rev. Mr Butler of the Presbyterian Mission in Ningpo, "they had to be appeased by the yearly offering of a girl of fair appearance and perfect body. At last one of the *literati* determined to stop this. He armed himself and jumped into the water; blood rose to the surface. He had killed one of the dragons. The other retired to the narrow place. A temple was erected to the hero at Peach Blossom ferry."[3]

In Japan[4] one of the dragon legends recounts how a very large serpent with eight heads and eight tails came annually and swallowed one person. A married couple who had eight children have at last only one girl left. They are in great grief. The hero, *So-sa-no-o no mikoto*, went to the sources of the river Hi-no-ka-mi at Idzumo and found an old man and woman clasping a young girl. "If you will give that girl to me I will save her." The mikoto changed his form and assumed that of the girl: he divided the room into eight divisions, and in each placed one saki tub. The serpent approached, drank the saki, got intoxicated, and fell asleep, whereupon the mikoto drew

---

[2] J. E. Hanauer's *Folk-Lore of the Holy Land*, p. 56. Arculf's stories of St George, learned in Constantinople, reached Iona in the seventh century (v. Adamnan: *De Sanctis Locis*).

[3] Gould's Mythical Monsters, p. 306 (London: W. H. Allen & Co., 1886). As a naturalist, this writer considers the dragon no mere offspring of fancy, but infers it to be a long terrestrial lizard, with much in common with *Draco volans, Moloch horridus*. Fond of bathing and basking in the sun. Habitat, highlands of Central Asia. For the rest he gives interesting accounts by Mr Maclean, minister of Eigg, in 1809, and by Mr Macrae, minister of Gleneig, in 1872, of the so-called Norwegian Sea-Serpent in the West Highlands.

[4] *Cf.* Campbell's Circular Notes, I., 326.

his sword and cut the serpent into pieces! Which proves the unwisdom of the Japanese serpent in drinking saki, and the observant mind of So-sa-no-o!

In China the dragon is the emblem of imperial power: a five-clawed dragon is embroidered on the Emperor's robes, with two legs pointing forwards and two backwards. Sometimes it has a pearl in one hand and is surrounded with clouds and fire. The chief dragon is thought to have its abode in the sky, whence it can send rain or withhold it. Its power is symbolised in the Emperor.

Literature abounds in references to dragon-monsters. Homer describes the shield of Hercules as having the scaly horror of a dragon coiled, with eyes oblique, that askant shot gleaming fire. Ovid locates the dragon slain by Cadmus near the river Cephisus, in Bœotia. Arthur carries a dragon on his helm, a tradition referred to in the Faerie Queen. Shakespeare, too:—

> *"Peace, Kent;*
> *Come not between the Dragon and his wrath!"*

Ludd's dominion was infested by a dragon that shrieked on May-Day Eve. In Wales, St Samson is said to have seized the dragon and thrown it into the sea. Among the Welsh, indeed, a pendragon came to mean a chief, a dictator in times of danger. And if we surveyed the lives of the saints, it would be tedious to enumerate the number who figure as dragon-slayers—all of them active long ere the days of the modern Mediterranean shark!

Over the linguistic area covered by the Celtic branches of the Indo-European peoples, legends of contests with monsters have been current from early times. As to their origin, it is difficult to be certain as to how far they may have been transmitted from one people to another. Possibly external influence may be traced in the *Bruden Dâ Derga*, a Gadhelic text from about the eighth century, which speaks of

"In leuidán timchella inn domon"[5]
(The Leviathan that surrounds the world).

The Cymric book of Taliessin tells of

---

[5] Leabhar Na h-Uidhri, 85*b*.

*"That river of dread strife hard by terra [earth],
Venom its essence, around the world it goes."[6]*

The Early Lives of the Saints have parallel references. In an eighth-century chronicle concerning St Fechin, we hear of evil powers and influences whose rage is "seen in that watery fury, and their hellish hate and turbulence in the beating of the sea against the rocks." Pious men are often afraid to approach the shore, fearing to encounter the like hellish influence. Of a great storm we read of "the waves rising higher and higher—Satan himself doubtless assisting from beneath."[7] The Life of the Irish Saint Abban tells how from his ship he saw a beastly monster on the sea, having a hundred heads of divers forms, two hundred eyes, and as many ears; it extended itself to the clouds and set the waters in such commotion that the ship was almost lost. The sailors feared greatly. St Abban prayed against the monster, the beast fell as if dead, and there was a calm. But strange to relate, the body of the monster could be seen neither on sea nor on land (*et in hoc apparet quod dyabolus fuit*).[8] In Adamnan's Life of Colum-Cill[9] there is a chapter concerning the repulse of a certain aquatic monster (*aquatilis bestia*) by the blessed man's prayer. The incident occurred somewhere by the river Ness. The inhabitants were burying one who had been bitten while swimming. To fetch a coble from the opposite bank, one of Columba's companions, Lugne Mocumin, cast himself into the water. And Adamnan relates:—

"But the monster, which was lying in the river bed, and whose appetite was rather whetted for more prey than sated with what it already had, perceiving the surface of the water disturbed by the swimmer, suddenly comes up and moves towards the man as he swam in mid-stream, and with a great roar rushes on him with open mouth, while all who were there, barbarians as well as brethren, were greatly terror-struck. The blessed man seeing it, after making the Salutary sign of the cross in the empty air with his holy hand upraised, and invoking the name of God, commanded the ferocious monster,

---

[6] Rhys, *Arthurian Legend*, 157

[7] *Nineteenth Century*, March 1895, p. 422.

[8] *Vitae Sanctorum Hiberniae*, ed. Plummer, Tomus Primus, p. 15.

[9] Bk. II., c. 27 (trans. W. Huyshe). For a dragon contest, see Nennius,. *Historia*, xl.-xlv

saying: 'Go thou no further, nor touch the man; go back at once.' Then, on hearing this word of the saint, the monster was terrified, and fled away again more quickly than if it had been dragged off by ropes, though it had approached Lugne as he swam so closely that between man and monster there was no more than the length of one punt pole."

The whole incident reflects some natural fact, together with the human belief in the possible occurrence of such. "The belief," says Bishop Reeves, "that certain rivers and lakes were haunted by serpents of a demoniacal and terrible character was current among the Irish at a very remote period, and still prevails in many parts of Ireland." St Molua and St Colman of Dromore are recorded to have saved people from such monsters. As to the modern Irish belief, let Mr W. R. Le Fanu's *Seventy Years of Irish Life* be evidence:—

"The dreadful beast, the wurrum—half fish, half dragon—still survives in many a mountain lake—seldom seen, indeed, but often heard. Near our fishing quarters in Kerry there are two such lakes, one the beautiful little lake at the head of the Blackwater River, called Lough Brin, from Brin or Bran as he is now called, the dreadful wurrum which inhabits it. The man who minds the boat there speaks with awe of Bran; he tells me he has never seen him, and hopes he never may, but has often heard him roaring on a stormy night. On being questioned what the noise was like, he said it was like the roaring of a young bull.' ... Some miles further on, between Lough Brin and Glencar, there is another lake from which a boy while bathing was driven and chased by the dreadful wurrum which dwells in it. It bit him on the back and hunted him all the way home, where he arrived naked and bleeding."

In the Life of St Mochua of Balla it is recounted that no one ventured to pursue a wounded stag that fled to an island in Lough Ree, on account of a horrible monster that infested the lake and was wont to destroy swimmers. A man was at last persuaded to swim across, but as he was returning the beast devoured him.

In the *Altus* of St Colum-Cille he refers to a great slimy dragon, terrible and most horrible, that slimy serpent more subtle than all the beasts:—

"Draco magnus deterrimus terribilis et antiquus qui fuit serpens lubricus sapientior omnibus bestiis... ."

Nor is a similar belief yet extinct in the Highlands. The late Miss Dempster of Skibo records in her manuscript a legend of St Gilbert and the Dragon, with a note that some say that this was not a dragon, but a witch from Lochlin—a variant to be expected in Sutherland:—

"There lived once upon a time in Sutherland a great dragon, very fierce and strong. It was this dragon that burnt all the fir woods in Ross, Sutherland, and the Reay country, of which the remains, charred, blackened, and half-decayed, may be found in every moss. Magnificent forests they must have been, but the dragon set fire to them with his fiery breath, and rolled over the whole land. Men fled from before his face, and women fainted when his shadow crossed the sky-line. He made the whole land desert. And it came to pass that this evil spirit, whom the people called the 'beast' and 'Dubh Giuthais,'[10] came nigh to Dornoch as near as Lochfinn, and when he could see the town and spire of St Gilbert, his church—'Pity of you, Dornoch,' roared the dragon. 'Pity of you, Dornoch,' said St Gilbert, and taking with him five long and sharp arrows, and a little lad to carry them, he went out to meet the 'beast.' When he came over against it he said, 'Pity of you,' and drew his bow. The first arrow shot the beast through the heart. He was buried by the towns-people. Men are alive now who reckoned distance by so or so far from the 'stone of the beast' on the moor between Skibo and Dornoch. The moor is planted, and a wood called Carmore waves over the ashes of the destroying dragon."

This church, Miss Dempster notes, was built between 1235-45, burnt 1570, and rebuilt 1614; it was repaired in 1835 by the Duchess, Countess of Sutherland. While the work was going forward the tomb of the founder, Gilbert, Bishop of Caitness, called St Gilbert, was discovered. The saying went in Sutherland that when this happened, the cathedral would fall at mid-day the following Sunday; and Mrs Dempster well remembered seeing a third of the congregation (Gaelic) camped out on the hill above the town, expecting to see the fall of the roof; nor did many of the oldest inhabitants go to church for several following Sundays.

---

[10] There is still an old pronunciation with *t* hard, and not *th*.

In addition to legends of the *beithir-nimh* (venomous serpent) and *uile-bheist* (dragon; also *a' bheisd)*, there are endless tales of the water-horse (*each-uisge*) associated with Highland lochs. There is hardly a district without some legend of a *Linne na Baobh* (Badhbh): very often the water-horse is represented as a kind of creature covered all over with rags and ribbons, typifying the wind-tossed surface of the waves. His appearance is a portent of a drowning soon to follow.

I n the poem of *Tristan and Iseult*, by Gottfried of Strassburg, a German poet who wrote about the year 1210, working on sources found by him in a poem by Thomas of Brittany, there is an account of the fight with the dragon, strangely analogous to that in Highland tradition. The hero overcomes a monster, and is about to be robbed of the credit of his exploit by a traitor who claims the princess as his guerdon. It is a widespread Aryan tale. A similar adventure is ascribed to Lancelot in *Le cerf au pied blanc*, and in the Dutch poem of *Morien*. At least three of the printed prose versions of Tristan retain the dragon fight,[11] whether it formed originally a part of the tale or not. Gottfried of Strassburg introduces it thus:—

"Now, the story tells us that there was at that time in Ireland a monstrous dragon which devoured the people and wasted the land; so that the king at last had sworn a solemn oath that whoever slew the monster should have the Princess Iseult to wife; and because of the beauty of the maiden and the fierceness of the dragon, many a valiant knight had lost his life. The land was full of the tale, and it had come to Tristan's[12] ears, and in the thought of this had he made his journey.

"The next morning, ere it was light, he rose and armed himself secretly, and took his strongest spear, and mounted his steed, and rode forth into the wilderness. He rode by many a rough path till the sun was high in the heavens, when he turned downwards into a valley, where, as the geste tells us, the dragon had its lair. Then he saw afar off four men galloping swiftly over the moor where there was no road. One of them was the queen's

---

[11] Löseth, *Le Roman en prose de Tristan*. For variants of the dragon fight, *v.* Hartland's *Legend of Perseus*, vol. iii.

[12] Tristan and his uncle Mark, Zimmer thinks, are ninth-century Pictish chieftains. Iseult he takes to be the daughter of the Viking King of Dublin.

seneschal, who would fain have been the lover of the Princess Iseult, but she liked him not. Whenever knights rode forth bent on adventures, the seneschal was ever with them for nothing on earth save that men might say they had seen him ride forth, for never would he face the dragon, but would return swifter than he went.

"Now, when Tristan saw the men in flight he knew the dragon must be near at hand, so he rode on steadily, and ere long he saw the monster coming towards him, breathing out smoke and flame from its open jaws. The knight laid his spear in rest, and set spurs to his steed, and rode so swiftly, and smote so strongly, that the spear went in at the open jaws, and pierced through the throat into the dragon's heart, and he himself came with such force against the dragon that his horse fell dead, and he could scarce free himself from the steed. But the evil beast fell upon the corpse and partly devoured it, till the wound from the spear pained it so sorely that it left the horse half-eaten, and fled into a rocky ravine.

"Tristan followed after the monster, which fled before him, roaring for pain till the rocks rang again with the sound. It cast fire from its jaws and tore up the earth around, till the pain of the wound overcame it, and it crouched down under a wall of rock. Then Tristan drew forth his sword, thinking to slay the monster easily, but 'twas a hard strife, the hardest Tristan had ever fought, and in truth he thought it would be his death. For the dragon had as aids smoke and flame, teeth and claws sharper than a shearing knife; and the knight had much ado to find shelter behind the trees and bushes, for the fight was so fierce that the shield he held in his hand was burnt well-nigh to a coal. But the conflict did not endure over-long, for the spear in the vitals of the dragon began to pain him so that he lay on the ground, rolling over and over in agony. Then Tristan came near swiftly and smote with his sword at the heart of the monster so that the blade went in right to the hilt; and the dragon gave forth a roar so grim and terrible that it was as if heaven and earth fell together, and the cry was heard far and wide through the land. Tristan himself was well-nigh terrified, but as he saw the beast was dead he went near, and with much labour he forced the jaws open, and cut out the tongue; then he closed the jaws again, and put the tongue in his bosom. He turned him again to the wilderness, thinking to rest through the day, and come again to his people secretly in the shadows of the night; but he was so overcome by the stress of the fight and the fiery breath of the dragon that he was well-nigh spent, and seeing a little lake near at hand into which a clear stream flowed from the rock, he went towards it, and as he came to the cool waters the weight of his armour and the venom of the dragon's tongue overpowered him, and he fell senseless by the stream.

"Iseult and her mother afterwards found Tristan, and drew him out of the water, whereupon the dragon's tongue fell from his breast. And when all the folk came together to know the end of the seneschal's matter, Tristan spake—

"'Lords all, mark this marvel, I slew the dragon, and cut this tongue from out the jaws, yet this man afterwards smote it a second time to death.'

"And all the lords said, 'One thing is clear, he who came first and cut out the tongue was the man who slew the monster.' And never a man said nay."[13]

Wales, too, has its legends of dragons, serpents, and snakes. It seems to have been an old Welsh belief that all lizards were formerly women.[14] Every Welsh farmhouse had two snakes. They never appeared until just before the death of the master or mistress of the house; then the snakes died." Parallel with this, perhaps, is the number of river names within the Celtic area that seem to contain the names of goddesses or nymphs of the stream. Such are met with in Lōchy, the Nigra Dea (black goddess) of Adamnan; in Affric, both a lake and river name, also a personal female name, from *aith bhric* (root), as in *breac* (spotted); in Nevis, where Dr MacBain rightly detected some nymph name like Nebestis; Aberdeen, Gaelic *Obair-dhea'oin*, with a strongly trilled *r*, showing that *dh* of old *deuona* (goddess, etc.) has been assimilated to the preceding word for estuary, deuona itself being a divine name, and exemplifying in a river name what Ausonius tells us was the case with sacred springs in Gaul—*fons addite divis* (they were dedicated to the gods) . To be included in the number is the name of the river Boyne, which under the form *Bofind* (white cow) yields Boyne, the name of Fraoch's mother's sister from the Sídh (Shee) or Faëry. The form Boand (genitive Bóinde), also that in the phrase *in (h)ostio Boindeo* (at the mouth of the

---

[13] From Gottfried von Strassburg's *Tristan and Iseult*, by J. L. Weston, I., 89, 98, 123. *Cf.* also Bedier's French retelling, Englished by Mr Belloc.

[14] Trevelyan, *Folk-Lore and Folk-Stories of Wales*, p. 165.

Boyne) goes back on some such form as Boouinda (white cow). This recalls an Irish name for the Milky Way—*bóthar bó finne* (the way or path of the cow of whiteness) . But in Uist I met with the name *Sliochd Uis* (Milky Way), meaning seemingly "the path or way of whiteness or brightness," the root of which recurs again in Uisne (Uisnech).

But the survey of the theme would not be complete in the form in which the more modern tradition leaves it. I have therefore given the story of Fraoch from the Book of the Dean of Lismore, and also the first part of the old and important tale known as the *Táin Bó Fráich*, of which the following manuscripts exist: The Book of Leinster; The Yellow Book of Lecan; Edinburgh Advocates' Library Gaelic MS. XL.; Egerton 1782 (British Museum). This old story has been edited with all the important variants, with his wonted care and skill, by Professor Kuno Meyer in the *Zeitschrift für Celtische Philologie* for 1902. In making my translation I tried to select from among the best of the variant readings. The last seven sections of the *Táin Bó Fráich* I have not translated here: they are apart from the Geste of Fraoch, and bring the hero of the narrative on further adventures elsewhere. This tale is one of the oldest of our secular narratives in Gadhelic: it belongs to about the ninth century, a period when the Scoto-Celtic idiom of Alba was one with the language of Erin. A translation was made by the late Mr J. O'Beirne Crowe, which appeared in the Royal Irish Academy Proceedings for 1870, but subsequent studies have necessitated many changes.

The name Fraoch (Fraech) is very ancient. It survives in the place name Clonfree (Cluain Fraeich), Strokestown, Roscommon. On an Ogham stone it occurs in *Netta Vroicci maqi muccoi Trenaluggo* at Donaghmore, Kildare; also in *Vraicci maqi Medvi* on an Ogham from Rathcroghan, Roscommon. In this last it stands for (the stone) of Fraoch, son of Medb.[15]   Another account of the death of Fraoch than that given in what I term the Geste of Fraoch is met with in the *Táin Bó Cuailnge*, where he meets his death at the hands of Cuchulainn. It is noticeable that his fairy origin is pointed to, and that his death is associated with water. This episode is at a later stage in his story than that in *Táin Bó Fráich*, which gives the serpent encounter. He had by this time accompanied Mève's forces as recounted in the Cattle-Raid of Cuailnge (*Táin Bó Cuailnge*), and his healing at the hands of the folk of

---

[15] MacAlister's *Irish Oghams*, pt. 3, p. 213; *Journ. Roy. Soc. Antiq. Ireland*, 5 ser.

Fiery is to be presupposed: here again they intervene, and we hear of Fraoch's fairy-mound. Here is the *Táin Bó Cuailnge* version of the death of Fraoch, or Fraech:—

"They are there till next morning; then Fraech is summoned to them. 'Help us, O Fraech,' said Medb (Mève). 'Remove from us the strait that is on us. Go before Cuchulainn before us, if perchance you shall fight with him.'

"He set out early in the morning with nine men, till he reached Ath Fuait. He saw the warrior bathing in the river.

"'Wait here,' said Fraech to his retinue, 'till I come to the man yonder; not good is the water,' said he.

"He took off his clothes, and goes into the water to him.

"'Do not come to me,' said Cuchulainn. 'You will die from it, and I should be sorry to kill you.'

"'I shall come indeed,' said Fraech, 'that we may meet in the water; and let your play with me be fair.'

"'Settle it as you like,' said Cuchulainn.

"'The hand of each of us round the other,' said Fraech.

"They set to wrestling for a long time on the water, and Fraech was submerged. Cuchulainn lifted him up again.

"'This time,' said Cuchulainn, 'will you yield and accept your life?'

"'I will not suffer it,' said Fraech.

"Cuchulainn put him under it again, until Fraech was killed. He comes to land; his retinue carry his body to the camp. Ath Fraich, that was the name of that ford for ever. All the host lamented Fraech. They saw a troop of women in green tunics[16] on the body of Fraech mac Idaid; they drew him

---

[16] W. Faraday's translation of The Cattle-Raid of Cuailnge, in Nutt's Grimm Library, p. 35. Fraech was descended from the people of the Sid, his mother Bebind being a fairy woman. Her sister was Boinn (the river Boyne).

from them into the mound. Sid Fraich was the name of that mound afterwards."

Ailill's plan in compassing the death of Fraoch recalls his episode with Fergus, son of Rōg. Keating[17] tells how, when Fergus was in banishment in Connaught, it happened that he was with Ailill and Mève in Magh Ai, where they had a fortress; and one day, when they went out to the shore of a lake that was near the *lios* (or outer court), Ailill asked Fergus to go and swim in the lake, and Fergus did so. While swimming, Mève was seized by a desire of swimming with him; and when she had gone into the lake with Fergus, Ailill grew jealous, and he ordered a kinsman of his to cast a spear at Fergus, which pierced him through the breast; and Fergus came ashore on account of the wound caused by that cast, and extracted the spear from his body and cast it in the direction of Ailill; and it pierced a gray hound that was near his chariot, and thereupon Fergus fell and died and was buried on the shore of the same lake.

Rhys points out that Ailill (written Oilill in Keating) seems cognate with Welsh *ellyll* (an elf or demon), and that Mève's Ailill belongs to a race which is always ranged against the Tuatha Dé Danann. Mève he associates with the goddesses of dawn and dusk, who are found at one time consorting with bright beings and at another with dark ones, and they commonly associate themselves with water. Curious too that Mève's sisters Eithne and Clothru are associated the one with the river Inny (Eithne) in Westmeath, the other with Clothru's Isle (Inis Clothraun) in Loch Ree.

Eochaidh Feidhlioch, monarch at Tara, was Mève's father. He had three sons and three daughters—namely, Breas and Nar and Lothar, the three sons; Eithne Uathach, Clothra, and Mève of Cruachan, the three daughters, as the poet says in this quatrain:—

"Three daughters had Eochaidh Feidhlioch,
*   Fame on a lofty seat:*
Eithne Uathach, fair Mève of Cruachan,
*   And Clothra."*[18]

---

[17] Ed. Dinneen, ii., 209.

[18] Dinneen's Keating, ii., 215.

O'Curry remarks of Mève that she seemed more calculated to govern many men than to be governed by one man. She soon abandoned Conchobar, and returned to her father, the monarch Eochaidh Feidhlioch, to Tara, who shortly after set her up as the independent queen of the province of Connaught. Through jealousy and hatred, fierce war raged between her and her former husband, Conchobar, who finally was killed by a Connaught champion, Cét Mac Magach. This Conchobar, King of Ultonia, is spoken of as being a terrestrial god among the Ultonians. His mother's name was Ness, hence he is known as Mac Nessa. This goddess name is connected with that in Loch *Ness*, and points to her as having been conceived of at first as a water-nymph. This does not prejudice what reflex of historic movements these stories may imply. Curiously, the death of Mève, no less than that of Fraoch, is associated with water. Keating's[19] account is as follows:—

"When Olill had been slain by Conall Cearnach, Mève went to Inis Clothrann, on Lough Ribh (Ree), to live; and while she resided there, she was under an obligation (*ba geis di, i.e.* under a taboo or *gessa*) to bathe every morning in the well which was at the entrance to the island. And when Forbuidhe, son of Conchobar (her former husband) heard this, he visited the well one day alone, and with a line measured from the brink of the well to the other side of the lake, and took the measure with him to Ulster, and practised thus: he inserted two poles in the ground, and tied an end of the line to each pole, and placed an apple on one of the poles, and stood himself at the other pole, and kept constantly firing from his sling at the apple that was on the top of the pole till he struck it. This exercise he practised until he had grown so dexterous that he would miss no aim at the apple. Soon after this there was a meeting of the people of Ulster and Connaught at both sides of the Shannon at Inis Clothrann; and Forbuidhe came there from the east with the Ulster gathering. And one morning, while he was there, he saw Mève bathing, as was her wont, in the fore-mentioned well; and with that he fixed a stone in his sling and hurled it at her, and struck her in the forehead, so that she died on the spot, having been ninety-eight years on the throne of Connaught, as we have said above."[20]

---

[19] Ed. Dineen, ii., 213. C

[20] But see Book of Leinster, 1246, 125a, where the story differs considerably from that given by O'Curry, who evidently quoted Keating.

Of Fraoch's mother Boand, elsewhere spoken of as from the Sídhe, the Bodleian Dindshenchus gives the following account:[21]—

"Bóann, wife of Nechtán, son of Labraid, son of Nama, went with the cupbearers to the well-of-the-green of the fortress. Whoever went alone to it came not from it without disgrace. Now these were the names of the cupbearers whom Nechtán had, even Flesc and Lesc and Luam. Unless the cupbearers went to the well, no human being would come from it without disgrace.

"Then, with pride and haughtiness, the queen went alone to the well, and said that it had no secret or power unless it could disgrace her shape. And she went round the well withershins thrice, to perceive the well's magic power. Out of the well three waves break over her, and suddenly her right thigh and her right hand and her right eye burst, and then she fled out of the fairy mound, fleeing the disgrace and fleeing the well, so that she reached the sea with the water of the well behind her. And the Inber Bóinne (river-mouth of Boyne) drowned her. Hence 'Bóann' and 'Inber Bóinne.'"

"One day Boyne of the mark of Bregia
Broke every fence as far as the White Sea;
Bóann was the name on that day
Of the wife of Nechtán, son of Labraid."

Nechtán, the mythic owner of the fairy precinct now called Trinity Well, into which one could not gaze with impunity, and from which the river Boyne first burst forth in pursuit of the lady who insulted it, may be cognate, Rhys thought, with Neptune, which certainly seems cognate with Irish Nuada *Necht*.[22]

---

[21] Trans. by Stokes, p. 34 of reprint from *Folk-Lore*, iii., 1892. Bóann p. xxxv now the river Boyne, which rises at the foot of Síd Nechtain, a hill in the barony of Carbury, co. Kildare. The story is versified in the Book of Leinster, 191a. See also Rhys, *Hibbert Lectures*, pp. 123, 556. The origin of rivers and lochs is often ascribed to mortals intruding upon secret wells. Truth lies deep at the bottom of a well, and in allegory will not be gazed upon. It is enough to eat of the fruit of the tree which is nourished by the spring.

[22] Rhys, Hibbert Lectures, 123.

How rivers came to be personified may be illustrated by an enigma which a poet puts to Finn in the tale of the Fairy-Palace of the Quicken Trees:[23]—

"I saw to the south a bright-faced queen
With couch of crystal and robe of green;
A numerous offspring sprightly and small,
Plain through her skin you can see them all;
Slowly she moves, and yet her speed
Exceeds the pace of the swiftest steed!
Now tell me the name of that wondrous queen,
With her couch of crystal and robe of green. "

To this Finn answers: "The queen you saw is the river Boyne, which flows by the south side of the palace of Bruga. Her couch of crystal is the sandy bed of the river; and her robe of green the grassy plain of Bregia, through which it flows. Her children, which you can see through her skin, are the speckled salmon, the lively pretty trout, and all the other fish that swim in the clear water of the river. The river flows slowly indeed; but its waters traverse the whole world in seven years, which is more than the swiftest steed can do."

A booklet entitled *The Death of Fraoch*, a Gaelic poem, was printed at Iona in 1887, by J. MacCormick and W. Muir, and published there by F. Ritchie. In 1888 a copy of the same appeared at Iona, with illustrations by W. C. Ward. For a perusal, after my own rendering was finished, of these now rare editions I have to thank Mrs MacMillan, the Manse, Iona. The Preface is of special interest, as telling that the events narrated "occurred in Mull, in the district surrounding Loch Laich.... The local tradition is that Fraoch lived at Suidhe, near the village of Bunessan. Opposite him, in an oblique direction on the other side of the loch, lived Mev, through whose treachery Fraoch was slain; the place is still known as *larach tigh Meidhe*. The island where the rowan tree grew is called after her, Eilean Mhain[24] (the isle of Main). It is right opposite to Bunessan.

---

[23] Joyce's Old Celtic Romances, 2nd ed., p. 587.

[24] *Cf.* Maine, son of Ailill, in the Táin Bó Cuailnge, folio 66*b*, 67*a*, 69*a* of facsimile of *Book of the Dun Cow.*

"The local tradition asserts that the monster which guarded the rowan tree, and by which Fraoch was slain, was a great serpent; but we take leave to doubt this, because great serpents were not known in Scotland. We think that the creature was the *torc nimhe* (wild boar), which undoubtedly was common in the Highlands. Some who possess the tradition say that Fraoch was found dead with the heart of the beast in his hand, on the strand of the 'Bay of the heart' (*Camus A' Chridhe*). The bay is there to witness this, but we do not read in the poem that the monster's heart was really torn out." The writers take exception to translating *Cruachan* in the third verse by Ben Cruachan, Loch Awe, and simply render *cruachan soir* "the hill in the east." They hope this rendering "effectually" dissipates "that myth"—*i.e.*, of associating the scene with Loch Awe. They have no recollection of the celebrated Cruachan in Roscommon. Fraoch they associate with *energy:* "Fraoch is seen to be an appropriate name for an eager, impetuous, generous, affectionate, strong, young man." The writers add that the strength of Fraoch is still proverbial. It is common yet to say *nam bithinn-sa cho làidir ri Fraoch spionainn craobh as a bun*—*i.e.*, "were I as strong as Fraoch, I could pull a tree from its roots."

A tune is added "as it was sung in Mull fifty years ago," on the authority of Mr Neil MacCormick of Fionn-phort—the first verse being repeated after each of the others, as a chorus. "It has the strain of a lament, and the tune to which it is sung is most melodious and melancholy." The air there noted is different to that given in the Appendix to Dr K. N. Macdonald's *Gesto Collection*. In Scotland the legend is also localised at Loch Freuchie, near Amulree, Perthshire; and at Loch Awe, Argyll, where the legend has been moralised in poetic treatment at the hands of Mr P. G. Hamerton in his *Isles of Loch Awe* (1855). Mr Hamerton compares the Celtic Myth to that of Hercules: he depicts both Fraoch and the lady as dying after the tasting of the poisonous fruit:

"Both their faces were in deepest shade
Close to each other. Thus the pair were found."

Mr Hamerton draws a moral:

"There are fables full of truth
Fraoch's tale is sadly true!

For how many in their youth,
Bitten by the serpent's tooth,
Die or only live to rue!"

A free rendering of the eighteenth-century Lay of Fraoch, which really does not belong to the Ossianic Cycle, was given by Jerome Stone, (1727-1756) in the *Scots Magazine*, with a letter dated Dunkeld, Nov. 15, 1755. He made an unwarrantable change in heading the poem *Sir Albin and the Daughter of Mey*.

In Hamerton the fruit is poisonous: Fraoch and the "Lady of Loch Awe" both die of it. The eating of the fruit of the Tree of Life brings death. Medb could not live without the fruit; Fraoch could not taste of it, or even go through the perils of getting it, without dying. Fraoch must not go near the water; otherwise there will be a conflict which will issue in his death. Boand (Boyne), his mother's sister, cautions Fraoch's mother against the water, according to a poem in the *Book of Fermoy*—

"Let him not swim Black Water,
For therein he shall shed his blood."

According to the Highland Lays, Fraoch dies by the serpent, and Findabair laments him. In the *Táin Bó Fraich* there is only a promised betrothal with Findabair. According to the *Book of Fermoy*, his wife is Treblann, a foster-child to Coirpre mac Rossa, who belonged to Faëry. In the *Táin Bó Fráich* his healing came from the Sídhe, and he survived to take part with Medb on the foray of the *Táin Bó Cuailnge*, when he fell at the hands of Cuchulainn. In either case his death is connected with water. Medb was previously wife of Conchobar, who, according to a gloss in the *Book of the Dun Cow*, was formerly a god upon earth (*día talmanda*). In another account we find Conchobar as the name of a river.[25] Medb's first husband would thus seem to have been a water-god. One might hazard the suggestion that in old Druidic teaching, Medb herself may have been a sort of sea-mother, if indeed their thought on ultimate things may have got the length of postulating a mother

---

[25] *Rev. Celtique*, 6, 173. With Conchobar's mother Ness, apparently seen as a goddess-name in Loch Ness, compare the Attic-Bœotian dialect Netos-Nessos: λίμνη Νεσσωντίς in Thessaly. And compare Hesiod, *Theog.* 341.

of mankind. The berries for which she craved were from the Tree of Life, the food of the gods, the eating of which by mortals brings death. Rowan hurdles were used in Druidic divination:[26] the rowan was a magic medicine; a monster was thought to haunt the roots of a rowan, and typified the guardian spirit of the tree. The thought is old among the Celts; on the second altar of Notre Dame there is a figure of the Celtic Hercules killing a serpent,[27] which the late Monsieur D'Arbois de Jubainville tried to explain by episodes from Gadhelic myth. The dragon may be thought of as the confiner that holds captive the fruit-bearing Tree of Life. On this view he may be the winter-monster which Hildebrandt sees in the Indian Vritra, the "confiner" that holds captive the rivers, while Indra is the spring or summer sun which frees them from the clutches of the winter dragon. The rage of the sun-god may be conceived of as manifested against the cloud-dragon, or the winter-dragon, or the sea-dragon. Fraoch may thus be the Celtic Hercules Furens, the name being the same in root as *fraoch* (wrath), early Irish *fraech* (fury, rage), which is cognate with Cymric *gwrug*.[28] His quest may be a solar journey; and he is swallowed by the monster as the sun is swallowed by the sea. On this view the dragon myth should portray the hero as being devoured by a fish, as on Semitic ground, for which the reader should consult the great Bible Dictionaries, which treat of Bel and the Dragon and allied themes. In *Fraoch* the hero is slain, which is parallel to his being swallowed by the sea; if not cast up again, he is healed at the hands of the Sídhe. May we not infer that the myth is an endeavour to shadow forth some aspects of the external world, a picture, not yet moralised, of the cosmic process, an eternal tragedy of nature?

So far as Fraoch's conflict is comparable with that of Herakles and the Hydra, I should like to emphasise a trait in Euripides (Ion, v. 192) where Herakles kills the hydra with golden sickles: Λερναῖον ὕδαν ἐναιρει χρυσέαις ἅρπαις ὁ Διὸς παῖς. On an Attic vase there is depicted the conflict of Herakles against the Centaur Nessos, in reality, a river-god. Perhaps if we

---

[26] For references, see Plummer's *Vitæ Sanctorum Hiberniæ*, I., cliv.

[27] S. Reinach, *Catalogue Sommaire du musée de Saint Germain*, p. 33, n. 354.

[28] For the Welsh, see Rhys, notes to *Twrc Trwyth*.

had the Celtic Myth in its earliest stage we should find Medb herself to have been a sort of serpent or water-monster.

The idea of a paradise or elysium among the Celts, as with the Greeks, assumes two aspects—either that of the hollow-hill (*sídhe*), that is, the fairy-mound, or that of the over-sea elysium. This contrast may have some relation to the civilisation and home of the Celts; the former pointing, as to its origin, to their continental home, the latter to their insular and maritime abode. The berries of the rowan tree are the berries of the gods, and as connected with the other world are parallel to the idea attached to Emain Ablach, Emain rich in apples, which, from the *Book of Fermoy* and from the *Voyage of Bran*, Professor Kuno Meyer has pointed out is connected with the Isle of the Blessed, and parallel to the idea attached to the Vale of Avalion (Avalon), where "falls not hail, nor rain, nor any snow." Underlying the whole is the idea of the Island of the Blessed, *insula promorum quae fortuna vocatur*. As to Fraoch's exploit, in so far as it may be parallel to that of Herakles, Wilamowitz-Moellendorff, in his Commentary on the Herakles of Euripides, has pointed out that the garden of the gods, with the tree which carries the apples of life, is really quite independent of the Herakles saga, while a highly archaic variant of that story is that Herakles leaps into the jaws of a sea-monster, the jaws of death. On Celtic ground, too, we have the contest of a hero with a water-monster quite apart from Fraoch, and the rowan tree guarded by the dragon. The continuation of the *Táin Bó Fráich* brings the hero across the sea to the Alps and to the Langobardi. Here Fraoch is represented as being of the Ultonians: after high exploits he and his friends came to the territory of the Cruithen-tuath, the Pictish people, and later on he joined Ailill and Medb on the *Táin Bó Cuailnge*. It is impossible to be sure whether we have not here a hint that Fraoch was a hero of the Picts, the people whom the Gael called Cruithne (Cruithen-tuath), a word cognate in root with Cymric *pryd* in Ynys Prydain, and pointing to the pre-Gadhelic population of these isles as a people who practised tatooing.

Apart from the accessory of the Tree of Life, the parallel that is closest of all is the rescue of Andromeda by Perseus. On a hydria in the Berlin Museum there is a representation of Perseus in conflict with the monster fish, where there is present Andromeda, Kepheus, and another woman (Jope?). The whole story of the Geste of Fraoch is there minus the rowan tree and the serpent, which is replaced by the monster fish. Among the Greeks it formed the subject of a lost drama of Euripides, but we know the theme from the pseudo-Apollodorus. Perseus, on having come to Æthiopia, the kingdom of Kepheus, found the king's daughter Andromeda about to be exposed to a sea-monster. Kassiepeia, the wife of Kepheus, had boasted of her beauty, and thus fell into strife with the Nereids, or water-nymphs. This brought on her the anger of the Nereids and of Poseidon, who sent a flood and a monster to her father's realm. The oracle of Ammon gave out that the disaster to the kingdom would be averted if the king abandoned his daughter Andromeda to be devoured of the monster. Pressed by the Æthiopians, Kepheus had his daughter bound to a rock; in this state she was found by Perseus, who, smitten with love, promised Kepheus to slay the monster on condition that he would have the king's daughter, on her deliverance, to be his wife. This condition was agreed to, and thereafter Perseus went to meet the monster, killed it, and rescued Andromeda. This is another version of the Herakles-Hesione saga, which briefly is as follows. Poseidon and Apollo came in human form to Laomedon, King of Troy, and promised, for a certain reward, to gird his city with walls. The king would not fulfil his promise when the work was ended; whereupon Apollo sent a pest, and Poseidon a sea-monster which used to carry off the people working on the fields. Laomedon sought the advice of an oracle, which counselled him, in penance for his guilt, to deliver his daughter Hesione to the monster. In consequence of this divine judgment, Hesione was chained to a rock. As Herakles came the way he offered to free the maiden if Laomedon would give him the horses which he formerly received from Zeus on account of Ganymede. Which being agreed to, Herakles slew the monster and freed the maid. But the stubborn king endeavoured to deceive Herakles also, which drew upon him the vengeance whereby Troy is said to have been first of all destroyed.

It is at Joppa, in Phoenicia, that the story of Andromeda has been localised of old. Pliny[29] tells us that the Phoenician Joppa is older than the flood, that it lies on a hill, in front of which is a rock where traces of the fetters of Andromeda are pointed out. And St Jerome, in his Commentary on Jonah, writes: "Here (at Joppa) is the place where on the strand are pointed out to

---

[29] *Natur. Hist.*, V., 13.

this day the rocks to which Andromeda was bound, and from which she is said to have been freed by the help of Perseus. And on an Attic vase is a representation of Jason being vomited from out of the belly of a sea-monster or dragon at the command of Athene."

While we have no reference as to Fraoch having been swallowed by the dragon, the fisher's first son was swallowed by the mermaid, who is induced from her love of music to cast him forth once more.[30] It is also noticeable that the impostor incident, so common in the dragon stories, alongside of the rescuer, is lacking in Fraoch. But the impostor incident must have been known of old among the Celts, for we find it alluded to in the Rescue of Derforgaill, or Dervorgoil, a variant of a folk-tale introduced into the "Wooing of Emer," a text of the Cuchulainn Cycle. On coming to the dwelling of Ruad, King of the Isles, at Hallowe'en, Cuchulainn hears wailing in the fort. The king's daughter Derforgaill has been assigned in tribute to the Fomori, and she is exposed on the seashore, awaiting their coming. Cuchulainn kills three Fomori (or sea-giants) in single combat, but his last opponent wounds him at the wrist. The girl gives a strip from her raiment to bind his wound, and her rescuer goes off without making himself known. "The maiden came to the *dūn* and told her father the whole story... . Many in the *dūn* boasted of having killed the Fomori, but the maiden did nor believe them." On a test having been applied, the maiden recognised Cuchulainn, it is to be inferred, from the piece from off her raiment on his wound.[31] In Brittany the impostor figures as a charcoal-burner, who professes to have killed the seven-headed serpent to which the king's daughter was to have been sacrificed, and he carries off the heads. But the herd had cut out the seven tongues, and these are tokens of the true victor.[32]

In Highland folk-tales the rescuer appears in the character of herd,[33] and the impostor as a squint-eyed,[34] carroty-headed cook. Its parallel in Ireland is

---

[30] Pp. 78-80 of Campbell's retelling.

[31] E. Hull, *The Cuchulainn Saga*, pp. 81-82 (trans. by K. Meyer.)

[32] Quoted in Hartland's *Legend of Perseus*, iii., 6.

[33] *Cf.* also MacInnes, Folk and Hero Tales from Argyll: *Lod the Farmer's Son* (properly the *Ploughman's* son, *aoirean;* Ir. *oireamh*, genitive *oireamhan* (ploughman); root as in L.

The Thirteenth Son of the King of Erin[35]; here the hero also hires himself as cow-herd, and rescues a king's daughter from an *úr-feist*, a great serpent of the sea, a monster which must get a king's daughter to devour every seven years. While he slept in the maiden's lap, she took three hairs from his head and hid them in her bosom. He has three conflicts with the monster, and each time he is victor. On the third trial the hero Sean Ruadh takes a brown apple, given him by a giant's housekeeper, and threw it into the monster's mouth, "and the beast fell helpless on the strand, flattened out, and melted away to a dirty jelly on the shore." The girl was able to identify her rescuer by one of his blue-glass boots. The hero finally put the claimants to death, and wedded the maid.

This story has been identified in Brittany and among the Basques. Mr E. Sidney Hartland says: "The indications point to a Celtic or Iberian population as the originators of the *Herdsman* type[36] ... a highly specialised type, differing considerably from any form of the classical story, and peculiar to the West of Europe. We have no direct evidence as to the date when the stories of the *Herdsman* type arose; but it will be recollected that there is reason to think the type belongs to the Celto-Iberian race, and therefore is of prehistoric age. Nor will the reader fail to note that the Rescue of Derforgaill (Dervorgoil, Dervorgilla) from the Fomori appears to be an offshoot of the same type that it is found among one of the branches of the same Celto-Iberian race, and that it is one of the oldest —nay, perhaps the oldest—post-classical variant in Europe of the Perseus group. All these considerations make for its independence of the classical tale; and their cumulative weight may fairly be called decisive."[37]

---

aro; Ir. *arathar* (plough); Welsh *arddwr*; E. *ear* (the soil). *Cf.* the racial name Eremon, Airem(on), with which Aryan has been compared, Skr. Arjaman.

[34] *Claon.* Hector Maclean's spelling claghann I would ask the reader to delete in favour of *claon*.

[35] Curtin, *Myths and Folk-Lore of Ireland*, 157; Larminie, *West Irish Tales and Romances*, 196; quoted in Hartland, *ibid.* iii., 4-6.

[36] Hartland, Legend of Perseus, iii., 10

[37] *Ibid.*, 177-178. I have already pointed out that Fraoch's own people are spoken of as the Cruithne (Picts), who may be supposed to have absorbed an Ivernian strain.

On this account alone the old story is worthy of a place in our esteem. It conduces to thought, if not to thoughtfulness. Whatever its full origin may be, I suggest that human sense-perception conjoined with racial memories of contest with the raw environment of Nature, and the memory of human ills entailed upon our race by monsters of the prime,[38] along with human phantasy and imagination acting upon the reports of sense, ought to be allowed their due claims to account for some moments of the tale. But folk-tales have a compound-complex origin. I am not in favour of needlessly multiplying hypotheses. Some moments may be due to other races. Nor ought we to close our eyes to the background of the heavens. If the berries from the rowan tree have aught in common with the golden apples of the Hesperides, fetched by Herakles, it is proper to recollect that worthy scholars read herein the remains of a saga connected with the moon. Siecke[39] explains that, according to some ancients, Herakles himself plucked the apples after he had slain the snake that guarded the tree; that he fetched the golden apple or the three apples from the extreme West, as was the case with the bull and the girdle of the Amazons. He holds that these are the expression of indubitable perceptions. "Who has not seen, where the sun declines, the golden horns of the bull, the golden girdle, the apple of gold?" says Siecke. All of them for a while had vanished, but Herakles brings them back; truly not forever; Athene or some other divinity will bring them to their place, and into the power of the dragon, for the World Order cannot be altered. Yet the hero kills the dragon anew, and fetches the golden apples once more. And so, I would add, with Fraoch.

There are dragons still to be slain. May the recital of an old tale kindle the mind to new adventures. Here are materials for poets and painters. It is we who are living now. Let us mould them to express ourselves. The ancients have expressed themselves through similar tales; nor will we fulfil ourselves by entirely disregarding our ancestral past and our wealth of complex tradition.

---

[38] Cf. H. N. Hutchinson, *Extinct Monsters* (Chapman and Hall, 1910). "But none of the giant reptiles of the secondary period were contemporary with man," observes Mr Hartland.

[39] *Drachenkämpfe*, Leipzig (Heinrich), 1907, p. 91.

Let me express my heartfelt thanks to Miss Rachel Ainslie Grant Duff, Delgaty Castle, for the kindness which prompted her to make beautiful illustrations for this book. It helps to make it so much more human, and has given me indefinable pleasure, which will communicate itself to other artists. And if anyone should paint Medb, let them remember an early description in the *Táin:* a beautiful, pale, long-faced woman, with long flowing golden-yellow hair, having a crimson cloak fastened with a brooch of gold over her breast, a straight-ridged spear flaming in her hand.

The theme is largely identical with that of St George and the Dragon, which meets us in the Golden Legend of Jacques de Voragine, and appears in the office books of the Church in the Middle Ages:—

"O Georgi Martyr inclyte
Te decet laus et gloria
Predolatum militia
Per quem puella regia
Existens in tristitia
Coram Dracone pessimo
Salvata est!"

THE GESTE OF FRAOCH

[*Wherein is told the hero's origin, his wooing of Find-abair, his killing of the monster that guarded the rowan-tree, and his betrothal.*]

1. Fraoch, son of Idad[40] of Connaught, was a son of Bébinn from the *Sídh*,[41] whose sister hight Boyne (*Bofind*). Of the heroes of Erin and of Alba the most beautiful man was he, save only that he was short-lived. Twelve cows his mother gave him from the *Sídh;* white with red ears were they. For seven years he kept household without taking to himself a wife. The number of his household was fifty princes, in age and dignity his equals, as to form and feature and bearing alike.

2. Find-abair, daughter of Ailill and Mève, from hear-say regarding him, gave him love, of which report was brought him at his place. Erin and Alba were full of his fame and story.

He accordingly bethought him of going to bespeak the girl, and then he talked of the matter with his folk. And his folk said: "Let word too be sent to thy mother's sister that she may give thee somewhat of raiment of the rare treasure of the *Sídh*.

---

[40] mē Idaid (Book of the Dun Cow, facsimile, p. 63[b], line 27); Idaith (Book of Leinster); Fiduig (Egerton, 1782); Idhaig (Edinburgh, MS. XL.); m[c] Fei[t] (Book of Dean of Lismore). Hence nominative Idad, genitive Idaid, the form of the oldest manuscript, seems preferable: it would readily yield the other variants in regular development. Fraoch may be pronounced as Fraech.

[41] Pronounce *Shee.*

3. To the sister Boyne (Bofind) he thereupon went to the plain of Bregia or Moy Breg. She gave him fifty mantles of dark blue, each for hue like to a beetle's back, with four black-grey brooch-rings on each, and each with a pin of red gold: with fifty pale white tunics having animal figures chased in gold. Also fifty silver shields edged with gold. For each man's hand a lance like to a candle such as befitted a palace,[42] each having fifty rivets of white-bronze, with knobs of burnished gold: the spear-points from below were of carbuncle inwrought, while the front irons of the spears were chased with precious stones, so that night shone as 'twere by the rays of the sun.

Further, fifty swords with hilts of gold, and for each rider a dark grey steed with bits of gold. Around each horse's neck was a plate of silver with bells of gold; fifty leather caparisons in purple with threads of silver, with buckles of gold and silver, and animal devices for ornament. Fifty whips in white bronze, with a golden hook on the handle of each. Seven grey-hounds in chains of silver, with an apple of gold a-piece, each having greaves of bronze. There was no colour which the hounds had not. Accompanying them in garments of diverse colours were seven trumpeters, with trumpets golden and silver, and golden pale yellow tresses, and they had plaids that glistened like the Shee. In front of them went three jesters having silver diadems and gilt about. Each had shields engraved with devices, with crested staves and ribs of white metal along the sides. Opposite them were three harpists, each of kingly presence. And in that guise they set out for Cruachan.

4. On coming into the Plain of Cruachan the watchman perceives them from the *Dūn*. And he spake:

"I behold a host coming towards the fort in their numbers; a troop more beautiful or splendid never came to Ailill and Mève since they assumed sovereignty, nor ever will. It is as if my head were in a wine-vat with the wind that goes over me: I have never seen the equal of the feats and frolic (the games and gestures) of the hero. His play-rods he casts with a shot from him, and the seven grey-hounds with their seven silver chains are at them ere they fall to earth.

---

[42] For brightness, *i.e.*

5. Then the folks came to view them from the *Dūn* of Cruachan, insomuch that they smother one another, and sixteen are killed while looking on.

On alighting at the door of the *dūn* they unyoked their horses and set loose the grey-hounds, which chase to Rath Cruachan seven hinds, seven foxes, seven hares, and seven wild boars, and these the youths kill on the lawn of the fort. Thereafter the dogs dashed into the Brei and caught seven others, which they deposited at the said entrance to the door of the chief *rath*, where Fraoch and his folk sat.

6. King Ailill sent word to them, and enquired whence they had come. They accordingly name themselves after their true names, which they gave.

"Here," said they, "is Fraoch, son of Idad."[43]

This the steward declares to the king and queen.

"An illustrious young hero," quoth Ailill, "let him come into the *Liss*."[44]

And quarters were allotted them.

7. The plan of the house was thus: seven apartments it had from fire to wall all around, decorated with gold, each with a fronting of bronze, and partition carvings of red yew variegated by fine planing withal. Three layers of bronze in the arched skirting of each apartment, with seven layers of brass from where the shields rested to the roof-tree. Of pine the house was made, and it had a covering of shingle on the outside. Sixteen windows it had with brass shuttings in each, and a brass yoke across the roof-light. Four beams of brass in the apartment of Ailill and Mève, all adorned with bronze and in the very centre of the house. Two silver frontings it had, and overlaid with gold; and by the fronting facing Ailill there was a silver wand that would reach the mid "hips" of the house, so as to command the inmates at all times and circuit the house all around from one door to the other. Having hung up their arms within, they make the circle of the house and were made welcome.

8. "Welcome are ye!" quoth Ailill and Mève.

---

[43] Mac Idhuidh—Egerton, 1782

[44] Outer court.

"It is for that we have come," quoth Fraoch.

"Not a journey for boasting shall this be," quoth Mève.

Thereafter Ailill and Mève arrange the chessboard. Fraoch then takes to playing chess with a man of their company.

The most beautiful of chess-boards it was: it had a board of white metal with four ear-handles, and gold edgings. A candlestick of precious stone gave them light. The chess-men were of gold and silver.

"Get ye food in readiness for the braves," quoth Ailill.

"That is not what I wish," quoth Mève. "I want to have a game with Fraoch."

"It liketh me well," quoth Ailill, "get up and go to him."

Mève then goes to Fraoch and at chess they play.

9. Fraoch's folk in the meantime were a-roasting the animals of the chase.

"Let thine harpers play for us!" quoth Ailill to Fraoch.

"Let them play in sooth!" quoth Fraoch.

Harp-bags they had of otter-skins mounted with ruby, adorned with gold and silver, and roe-skins, white as snow around the middle, with black-grey "eyes" in the centre. Gold and silver and bronze in the harps, which were chased with figures of serpents and birds and hounds in silver and gold. With the movement of the strings the figures would move all about. The harpers having played, twelve of Ailill and of Mève's folk died of sorrow and of grief.

10. Gentle and melodious this Triad; theirs were the chants of child-birth.[45] Three noble brothers were they: Sorrow-strain, Joy-strain, Sleep-strain, and Boyne from the Shee (*Sídhe*) their mother: it is of this music which Uaithne the Dagda's harp played that the three are named. What time children were being born its strain was sorrow and travail from the soreness of birth-pangs

---

[45] Uaithne

beginning; next a strain of glee and of joy it played because of the pleasure of bringing the two sons to the birth; the strain played by the last son was one soothing and soft because of the heaviness of birth, so that it is from him that the third of the music has been named.

Boyne then awoke out of sleep.

"I receive," she said, "thy three sons, O Uaithne of full ardour, since Sorrow-strain, Joy-strain, Sleep-strain are on kine and women who shall fall by Mève and Ailill. Men shall fall on hearing the strains being played."

Thereupon the playing ceased.

"Splendidly has it come off!" said Fergus.

11. "Apportion us the food," said Fraoch to his folk. "Bring it in."

Lothar, having stepped within, divides them the food. On his hand used he to divide each joint with his sword, leaving neither shred nor skin; since he took to dividing he never hacked the meat under his charge.

Three days and three nights, then, were Mève and Fraoch playing chess, by reason of the abundance of precious stones with Fraoch's folk. Thereafter Fraoch addressed Mève.

"Well have I played against thee: I take not thy stake from the chess-board that there be to thee no decay of honour."

"Since ever I have been in this *dūn*," said Mève, it is this day that I feel the longest."

"Yea, certainly indeed," quoth Fraoch, "three days and three nights have we been playing chess."

12. At this Mève starts up. She felt shame at the warriors being without food. And she goes and tells this to Ailill.

"An extraordinary deed have we done—the warriors outside who have arrived to be without food!"

"Dearer to thee is chess-playing," quoth Ailill.

"It hinders not food being distributed throughout the house to his suite. Three days and three nights are they there without our having perceived the night through the glare of the precious stones within."

"Tell them then," said Ailill, to cease the lamentations they make until food be served them."

Thereupon food is served them and it pleased them well; and they stayed there three days and three nights a-feasting.

And thereafter Fraoch was called to the hall of audience to converse with Ailill and Mève. They ask him his errand.

"It pleases me in sooth to visit you," said he.

Your company is indeed not displeasing to the household," said Ailill. "Your arrival is preferable to your departure.[46]"

"We shall stay with you another week, then," said Fraoch.

They stay until the end of a fortnight at the *dūn*; every day they go to the chase and hunt. And the men of Connaught used to come to view them.

13. It was, however, a trouble with Fraoch not to have converse with the daughter, for it was that "benefit" that had specially brought him.

Night at end he got up one day to bathe in the river. It was at the same time that she with her maid went to bathe.

He takes her hand. "Stay to speak with me, it is for thee I have come," he said.

"Pleased am I," said the girl, "but if I come I could do nothing for thee."

"Would'st thou not elope?" he queried.

"I will not elope," she said, "I am a king and queen's daughter. Thine estate is not so humble that thou would'st not get me from my people, and it is my choice too to go to thee, for it is thou whom I have loved. And do thou take

---

[46] Lit., "Your addition is better than your diminution."

this ring of gold with thee," said the girl, "and it shall ever be a token between us. My mother gave it me to put by; I will say that I mislaid it."

They each then part.

14. "I am fearing indeed," quoth Ailill, "the eloping of yon daughter with Fraoch.

"'Twere not in vain[47] even should she be given him; he would come to us with his cattle to aid us at the *Táin*," said Mève.

Fraoch goes to the audience chamber. "Is it a secret ye are speaking of?" he quoth.

"Though it were a secret, thou would'st fit in," said Ailill.

"Will ye give me your daughter?" said Fraoch.

"She will be given thee," said Ailill, "if thou give me her purchase-price[48] which I shall name."

"Thou shalt have it," said Fraoch.

"Sixty black-grey steeds to me," said Ailill, "with their bridle-bits of gold, and twelve milch-cows, each in milk, and each having a white red-eared calf; and do thou come to me with all thy force and with thy musicians for the bringing of the kine from Cuailnge—my daughter to be given thee provided thou dost come to the Hosting."

"I swear," Fraoch spake, "by my shield, by my sword, and by mine arms, I would not give that purchase-price even were it for Mève herself."

Then he marched out of the house.

15. Mève and Ailill thereafter fell to conversing within, and said:

---

[47] "Love's labour lost."

[48] Dowry from the bridegroom; *cf.* marriage-settlement.

"Should he carry off the girl he will bring a host of the Kings of Erin against us. What is good is, let us dash after him and slay him forthwith ere he work us ruin."

That were[49] a pity and a loss of honour to us," said Mève.

"It shall not be a loss of honour for us," said Ailill, "the way I shall prepare it."

16. Ailill and Mève go into the Palace.

"Let us set off," said Ailill, "that we may see the chase-hounds a-hunting until midday, until they are tired."

Thereafter they set off to the river to bathe themselves.

"Fraoch! I am told," said Ailill, "thou art expert in water; get into this *linn*[50] that we may behold thy swimming."

"What kind of *linn* is it?" said Fraoch.

"We know not any danger therein, and bathing in it is frequent," Ailill said.

Fraoch then strips off his clothes and goes into the *linn;* his girdle he leaves on shore. Ailill opens Fraoch's purse behind his back, and finds therein the gold ring, which Ailill recognises.

"Come here, O Mève!" said Ailill.

Then Mève goes to the place where Ailill was.

"Dost thou recognise that?" said Ailill.

"I do recognise it," said Mève.

Ailill casts the ring into the water.

---

[49] Lit., is.

[50] Pool.

Fraoch, however, perceived that, and saw how a salmon leaped to meet it and took it into his mouth. Fraoch made a dash for the salmon, caught it by the jowl, went to land and brought it to a hidden spot by the brink of the river. He then proceeded to come out of the water.

17. "Come not out of the water," said Ailill, "until thou bring me a branch from yonder rowan-tree that is on the brink of the river: beautiful I deem its berries."

He then goes off and breaks a branch from off the tree, and brings it on his back across the water. And the remark of Find-abair was:

"Is that not beautiful that ye see?" Beautiful she thought it to see Fraoch over the black linn:[51] the body of great whiteness, the hair of great loveliness, the face so well formed; the eye of deep grey, and he a tender youth without fault, without blemish; with his face small below and broad above; his build straight and flawless; the branch with the red berries between the throat and the white face. Find-abair was wont to say that she had not seen aught that would come up to him half or third for beauty.

18. Thereafter he throws them the branches out of the water. "Lovely and beautiful are the berries; bring us more of them."

He goes off again; as he was in the middle of the *linn*, the monster from out the water lays hold of him.

"Give me a sword," Fraoch cried, "The monster hath got hold of me."

There was not on land one who would dare give it to him for fear of Ailill and of Mève.

Thereupon Find-abair strips off her clothes and gives a leap into the water with the sword. Ailill casts a five-pronged spear at her from above, a shot's length, so that it passes through her two tresses of hair. Fraoch, however, caught the spear in his hand, shoots it to landwards, the monster all the while being in his side. It was a bow-cast, a species of champion's weapon-feat, so that it pierces Ailill's purple robe and tunic. Thereupon the young

---

[51] Eg. version adds: *in the Brei.*

braves who were in Ailill's suite got up. Find-abair then gets out of the water, and leaves the sword in Fraoch's hand. Fraoch cuts off the monster's head so that it lay above on its rump, and Fraoch brings the monster to land. From this is named *Duiblind Fráich*, Fraoch's Black-Linn (Black-Pool) on the Brei in the lands of the men of Connaught. Thereafter Ailill and Mève go to their *dūn*.

19. "A great deed we have done!" quoth Mève.

"Of what we have done to the man we repent," says Ailill, "for he is not to blame. As for the girl, on the other hand, her lips shall pale in death ere the morrow's eve, nor shall her guilt be the bringing of the sword. For this man do ye prepare a bath of fresh-bacon broth and heifer-flesh minced in it with adze and axe—Fraoch therein to be bathed." All that was done as he said.

20. Then the Horn-blowers (or Trumpeters) preceded Fraoch to the *dūn*, and such was their playing that thirty of Ailill's and of Mève's friends-in-chief die from the magic music.

Fraoch was led into the *dūn*, and brought into the bath. And the women-folk rise around him at the vat to rub him and to lave his head. On being brought out of it a bed was made.

Then was heard the sore lament from over Cruachan drawing nigh, and there were seen thrice fifty women in crimson tunics, with head-dresses of green, and silver rings on their wrists.

One is sent to them for tidings to learn why they keen.

"For Fraoch son of Idad" (*Fraoch mac Idhaidh*), spake the Banshee, "in south for the darling of the *Sídhe*—princess of Erin."

Thereat Fraoch hears that plaintive keen.

"Lift me out," said he to his folk, "this is the *keen* of my mother and of the ladies of Boyne."

Thereupon he is lifted and brought out to them. The women come around him and bring him off to the *Sídhe* (Shee) of Cruachan.

On the morrow at the ninth hour they saw him return, with fifty women around him, and quite whole. Flawless and stainless—the women being alike in age, shape, form, and loveliness, in beauty and symmetry and figure alike in appearance as the women of the Sídhe, so that there was no means of knowing the one from the other. Men all but smothered one another [as they pressed] around them, until in the door of the liss or outer court they separate. They raise their *keen* at departure, so that they set the men in the liss beside themselves. From this is named the Keen of the Banshee, a fairy-melody with the musicians of Erin.

21. Into the *dūn* goes Fraoch, and the hosts rise up before him, and bid him welcome as if it were from another world he came.

Ailill and Mève arise and show they are penitent for the misdeed they did him; they make full peace and betake themselves to feasting until night.

Fraoch summons a servant of his suite and said:

"Get thee off to the spot where I went into the water: a salmon I left there, bring it to Find-abair, and of it let herself take charge, and let her broil it well. The gold-ring is in the salmon's middle. I expect it will be asked of her to-night."

They become inebriated, and music and playing delight them.

22. Quoth Ailill to his steward: "Bring me all my treasures."

They were brought him and were before him.

"Wonderful, wonderful!" they all exclaimed.

"Call ye Find-abair to me," said Ailill.

With a train of fifty maidens she comes in.

"Well, daughter," Ailill spake, "the ring which I gave thee last year is it in thy possession? Bring it me that the warrior-braves may see it; thou shalt have it again."

"I do not know," she said, what has become of it."

45

"Well, find out," said Ailill, it must be sought, else the soul must part with thy body."

"It is unworthy to say so; there is much that is fine besides," said the warrior-braves. And Fraoch spake:

"I possess no treasure which I would not give up on behalf of the girl, for she has brought me the word to save my life."[52]

"Of treasures thou hast none which can save her if she bring not the ring back," Quoth Ailill.

"I have no power to give it," said the girl, do with me what thou wilt."

"By the god of my folk," said Ailill, thy lips shall pale in death if thou return it not. Why it is asked of thee is because of the impossible. Until the dead come back who died since the world began, from where it was flung I know it doth not return."

"Verily, not for reward or longing shall the wished for treasure return," said the girl. "Since, however, thou dost long for it so pressingly I go to bring it thee."

"Go, indeed, thou shalt not," said Ailill, but let some one go from thee to fetch it."

And the girl sent her maid. "I swear by my people's god," she said, "should anyone be found to protect me from the tyrant's stroke,[53] I shall no longer be in thy power should the ring be found."

Should the ring be found," said Ailill, "I shall certainly not prevent thee, should it even be with the groom (stable-boy) that thou should'st go."

23. The maid then brought into the palace the dish with the broiled salmon thereon, well prepared with honey dressing. Over the salmon lay the golden ring.

---

[52] Lit., in pledge for my soul.

[53] This rendering only paraphrases the original, where *sarol mogreiss* seems to convey the ideas of oppression and servility.

Ailill and Mève view it.

Let me see!" said Fraoch, "and he looked for his purse."

"Meseemeth, it is for a testimony that I left my girdle behind," said Fraoch. "Declare on thy Royal Word what thou hast done with the ring!"

"Yea I will not conceal it from thee," Ailill said. "Mine is the ring which was in the purse, and I knew it was Find-abair who gave it thee. On this account I flung it into the Black Linn. On thy word of honour, and by thy soul, declare O Fraoch, how it has happened to be brought out."

Fraoch spoke: "I will not conceal it from thee. On the first day I found the thumb-ring at the door of the Liss, and I knew it was a lovely gem; therefore I carefully put it by in my purse. On the day that I went to the water I heard how the girl had gone out to seek it. I said to her: 'What reward shall I have from thee for finding it?'

"She told me that she would give me a year's love. It chanced that I had not got it with me; I had left it behind me in the house. We met not until we met as she gave the sword into my hand in the river. And thereafter I saw when thou didst open the purse, and didst fling the thumb-ring into the water, and I saw the salmon spring to meet it so that it took it into its mouth. Then I caught the salmon, took it up on the bank and put it into the girl's hand. It is that salmon then which is on the dish."

24. At these tales the household were struck with astonishment and they marvelled.

"I shall not bestow my thought on another youth in Erin after thee," said Find-abair.

"Betroth thee to him," said Ailill and Mève, "and do thou come to us with thy kine to the raid of the kine of Cualnge: on thy return once more from the east with thy kine, ye twain shall wed that same night, thou and Find-abair."

"I will do so," Fraoch replied.

They are there until the following day, when Fraoch with his companions got ready and bade farewell to Ailill and to Mève. They then set out for their own bounds.

THE DEATH OF FRAOCH[54]

On Cluan Fraoich[55] a friend doth sigh
Where doth lie a warrior low
On his bier;
And his moan makes warriors grieve
And bereft of love his spouse.
For Idad's son she doth keen
For whom is named Cairn Laive:
Fraoch mac Idad of soft locks,
Idad's son of raven hair.
Westward there lies Fraoch mac Idad
Who fulfilled proud Mève's behest.
On Cruachan Shee (Sídh) a mother weeps:
Sad the tale—a mother's wail
She grieves sore for Fraoch her son.
Many a field in strifes of old
He had won and behold
Fraoch mac Idad lieth cold.

1. H-osnadh caraid an Cluan Fhraoich
H-osnadh laoich an caiseal chró
H-osnadh dheanann tuirseach fear,
Agus da'n guileann bean óg.

2. Aig so shear[56] an carp fa'n bh-feil
Fraoch mac Fhiodhaich an fhuilt mhaoith,
Fear a rinn buidheachas baoibh
Is bho'n sloinntear Carn Fraoich.

3. Gul aon mhna an Cruachan soir
Truagh an sgeul fa bh-feil a' bhean
Is se bheir a h-osnadh gu trom
Fraoch mac Fiodhaich nan colg sean.

4. 'Si 'n aon bhean do nidh an gul
Ag dol d'a fhios gu Cluan Fraoich,
Fionnabhair an fhuilt chais ail

---

[54] Retold after the Book of the Dean of Lismore, a sixteenth century text. The tale might be entitled: The Tree of Life in Gadhelic Legend. Its teaching might be summarised: Thou shalt not break off the branches from the Tree of Life, nor attempt to uproot it; in the day that thou disturbest it thou shalt surely die. Its guardian is the serpent, the Dragon-Snake (the Mother of Mankind possibly thus typified).

[55] Fraoch's mead, i.e.

[56] Shiar?

To Cluan Fraoich comes Find-abair:
She doth weep—a sad ladye;
With tresses soft and curling locks
And her hand
Of Queen Mève proud heroes sought.

Find-abair of golden hair
Ailill's one daughter she
Lies side by Fraoch to-night:
Of many loved, of many sought
But never a love
But Fraoch had Find-abair.

Her cause of hatred unprovoked Mève
found
For Fraoch the best of knights,
Bravest and friendliest:
When love for him she found
Her passion he did scorn
And hence his wound:
Fraoch lies a corpse to-night.
Great was the wrong thus wrought by
Mève:
Simply we still unfold
The story old:
(With woman-kind side not in ill)
His death her scheme foretold.
    (On Cluan Fraoich a friend doth sigh.)

A rowan tree grew on Loch Mève—
  Southwards is seen the shore—
Every fourth and every month
  Ripe fruit the rowan bore:
Fruit more sweet than honey-comb,
Its clusters' virtues strong,
Its berries red could one but taste
Hunger they staved off long.

Inghean Mhaoidhbh[57] g'am biaid
laoich.

5. Inghean Orla[58] as úr folt
   Is Fraoch an nochd taobh air thaobh
   Ge mór fear dha' dtairgeadh i
   Nior ghrádhaich si fear ach Fraoch.

6. Faigheas Meadhbh a muigh fuath
   Cairdeas Fhraoich fa fearr an gliadh,
   A' chúis fa'n chreuchd-ta a chorp
   Tre gun lochd a dhèanamh ria.

7. Do chuireadh e gu sa' bhás
   Taobh re mnaibh na tug an olc
   Is mór am pudhar a thuit le Meadhbh
   Inneósad gun cheilg a nos.
                    H-osnadh.

8. Caorrunn do bhi air Loch Mái,
   Do chidhmist an traigh fa dheas;
   Gach[a] ráidh [agus] gach mí,
   Toradh abaidh do bhi air.

9. Sásadh bídh na caora sin,
   Ba mhillse na mhil a bhláth;
   Do chongbhfadh an caorrann dearg
   Fear gun bhiadh gu ceann naoi tráth.

---

[57] *Recte* Maoidhbh.

[58] *Recte* Ailell'.

Its berries' juice and fruit when red
For a year would life prolong:
From dread disease it gave relief
If what is told be our belief.

Yet though it proved a means of life
  Peril lay closely nigh;
Coiled by its root a dragon lay
  Forbidding passage by.

A messenger for Fraoch was sent
  By Eochaidh's daughter keen—
When sickness sore Mève rent:
  "What ails?" quoth Fraoch, "the
Queen?"

And Eochaidh's daughter made reply—
  Eochaidh of the festive horns—
That ne'er would she be whole
  Till her soft palm were full
Of berries from the island in the lake—
  Fraoch's hand alone to pull.

"Such I ne'er cull'd," said Idad's son
  Of blushing face;
Yet will I what I yet ne'er willed,"
  Quoth Fraoch, out of grace.

Sir Fraoch moved forward to his fate
  Forth to the lake and swam the tide;
He found asleep the dragon-snake
  Around the tree, mouth open wide.
  (On Cluan Fraoich a friend doth sigh.)

10. Bliadhain air shaoghal gach fir
  Do chuireadh sin fa sgeal dearbh
  Gum bu fhóirinn do luchd cneidh
  Fromhadh a mheas is e dearg.

11. Do bhi anshástacht[59] 'na dhéigh
  Ge ba leigh a chobhar an t-sluaigh,
  Péist nimh do bhi 'na bhun[60]
  Bhacadh dha cách dhul d'a bhuain.

12. Léan easlainte throm throm
  Inghean Eochaidh nan corn saor,
  Do chuireadh fios leath air Fraoch,
  Dh' fhiosraich an laoch ciod thainig ri.

13. A dubhairt Meadhbh nach bi slán
  Mur faigh lán a boise maoith
  Do chaoraibh an locha fhuair
  Gun duine ga bhuain ach Fraoch.

14. Cnuasachd riamh ni dhearnadh mi
  Ar Mac Fiodhaich go ngné dheirg
  Ge gar dhéarnas e ar Fraoch
  Rachsad do bhuain chaor do
Mheidhbh.

15. Gluaiseas Fraoch, b'e fear an áigh
  Bhuain a shnámh air an loch
  Fhuair a' phéist is i 'na suain
  Is a ceann suas ris an dos.
          H-osnadh.

---

[59] Amsy = aimiseachd; aimsiughadh, "temptation": fascination? 'N aimcheist mhór a bha na dhiaidh (*Gillies; MacLagan*).

[60] A' Bheithir gharg is miosa nimh (Cameron's *Reliq. Celt.*, i., p. 225).

Fraoch, Idad's son, of weapon keen
  Of the beast being unperceived,
Of berries red a lapful brought
  Mève's longing to relieve.

Though good be that which thou hast
brought,"
  Quoth Mève of form so fair,
"Nought me relieves, O Champion bold
  Save branch from trunk thou bear."

Fraoch gave consent: no fear he knew
  But swam the lake once more:
But hero never yet did pass
  The fate for him in store.

The rowan by the top he seized
  From root he pulled the tree;
And the monster of the lake perceived
  As Fraoch from the land made free.

With his gaping maw the hero's hand
  He seized in the liquid tide:
Fraoch seized the monster by the jaw,
  Would a knife were by his side!

16. Fraoch mac Fiodhaich an airm ghéir
  Tháinig o'n phéist gun fhios di,
  Thug a h-anultach chaor dearg
  Far an robh Meadhbh dh' a tigh.

17. "Ach ge maith na tugais leat,"
  Adubhairt Meadhbh as geal cruth,
  "Ni fhóir mis, a laoich luain
  Ach slat a bhuain as a bun."

18. Togras Fraoch, 's nior ghille tiom,
  Shnámh a rís air an linn bhuig
  Is nior fheud [ne]ach[61] ge mór ágh
  Theachd o'n bhás an robh a chuid.

19. Gabhas an caorrann air bharr,
  Tharruing an crann as a fhrèimh,
  Tabhairt dó [a] chos do'n tór
  Mothaicheas do ris a' phéist.

20. Beireas air agus e air snamh,
  Is gabhas a lamh 'na craos,
  Do ghabh se-san is' air ghiall,
  Truagh gun an sgian aig Fraoch!

Find-abair of lovely tresses
  For Sir Fraoch her love,
Unperceived, a knife she bore;
  Fraoch's fair skin the monster tore
  And gnawing shore his arm away.

Fraoch, Idad's son, in conflict dire
  With the monster's woeful ire:
On the southern strand they fought and
fell

21. Fionnabhair an fhuilt chais áil
  Do ran chuige sgian gun fhoir,
  Liodair a' phéist a chneas ban
  Is theasgadh a lámh air leodh.

22. Do thuiteadar bonn re bonn
  Air traigh nan clach corr fo dheas;
  Fraoch mac Fiodhaich is a' phéist,
  Truagh, a Dhé, mar thug an treas!

---

[61] or, ach = howsoever.

And blood the boulders dyed.

Nor short the conflict: in his hand
  Fraoch held the monster's head;
Which when the maiden did perceive
  On the strand she swooned as dead.

The maid then spake as she awoke
  In her palm his hand she placed,
"Though now but food for birds-of-prey,
  Thy renown on earth is traced."

And from the death the hero died
  The lake doth take its name;
For ever is it hight Loch Mève,
  And thus resounds his fame.
    (On Cluan Fraoich a friend doth
sigh.)

His body to Cluan Fraoich is borne
  A hero on his bier laid low;
And still the mead his name makes
known
  Ah! pity the survivor's woe.

Cairn-of-the-Hand beside me here
  Is named from Fraoch Cairn Laive,
Back he ne'er turned his hand but fought
  The foremost when alive.

Belov'd the mouth that friends ne'er
scorned
  The lips which woman's lips had
pressed;
Belov'd the chief, of hosts the lord,
  Belov'd the cheeks the rosiest.

23. Ga cómhrag ni cómhrag géarr:
    Do rug leis a ceann 'na laimh;
    Nar chunnaic an nighean e
    Do chaidh 'na neul air an traigh.

24. Éir'eas an nighean o'n tamh,
    Gabhas an lamh, ba lamh bhog;
    Ge ta so 'na cuid nan eun[62]
    Is mór an t-euchd a rinn a bhos.

25. O'n bhás sin do fhuair am fear
    Loch Maidhbh gun lean de'n loch
    Ata an t-ainm sin deth gu luan
    'Ga ghairm a nuas gus a nos.
                    H-osnadh charaid.

26. Beirear an sin gu Cluan Fraoich
    Corp an laoich gu caisil chró;
    Air an gcluain tugadh a ainm
    Is mairg a mhaireas d[a éis beó].

27. Carn-laimh, an carn so re m' thaobh
    O laimh Fhraoich do bhidheast son,
    Fear nar iompodhadh an treas
    Fear ba dheise neart an trod.

28. Ionmhuinn am beul nar ob dáimh
    D'am bidis mnai a' toirbheart phóg
    Ionmhuinn Tighearna nan sluagh
    Ionmhuinn gruaidh nar dheirg an rós.

29. Duibhe na fitheach barr a fhuilt
    Deirge a ghruaidh na fuil laoigh
    Fa mhine na cobhar sruth

[62] na chodaibh éun (traditional variant).

53

Cheek redder than the blood of fawn
  Hair darker than the raven's crest,
And softer than the streaming foam,
  Whiter than snow Fraoch's waist.

More fringed than meadow-sweet his
locks,
  Than violet his eye more blue;
Than rowans ripe his lips more red,
  Whiter his teeth than woodbine hue.

Than mast his spear was higher; his
voice
More musical than lute:
  No swimmer that with Fraoch could
vie
His side by water put.

  Broader than door-leaf was his shield,
Whoso could wield it, happy lord!
  Long as his lance the arm of Fraoch
Than ship's plate more broad his sword.

Would that Fraoch by heroes bold,
  The bestower of gold—fell;
Alas and alas! through a monster's hold
  We hear his funeral knell.
        (On Cluan Fraoich a friend doth
sigh.)

Gile na an sneachd cneas Fhraoich.

30. Caise na an caisean 'fholt
Guirme a rosg na eidhr'-leac[63]
Deirge na partan a bheul
Gile a dheud na bláith feith.

31. Aird' a shleagh na cranna siúil
Binne na teud chiúil a ghuth
Snamhaidhe do b'fhearr na Fraoch
Cha do shín a thaobh re sruth.

32. Ba leithn' na comhla a sgiath
Ionmhuinn triath a bhi re druim
Co fad a lann is a lamh
Leithn' a cholg na clár dhe luing.

33. Truagh nach an comhrag re laoich
Do thuit Fraoch a phronnadh ór
Tuirs' sin a thuiteam le péist
Truagh, a Dhé, nach maireann fós.
        H-osnadh.

---

[63] Yr' lak (Dean of Lismore's spelling). A plant is apparently meant as in the other lines: *feith* "woodbine, honeysuckle (Hogan's Luibhleabhrán): *partan*, "berry of the mountain ash" (*ib.*, p. 60).

THE

CELTIC

DRAGON

MYTH

INTRODUCTION TO THE CELTIC DRAGON MYTH

1. At some time of the world, long long ago, there lived a poor old smith whose name was Duncan, and he lived in a little hut by the sea-shore. His house was built of boulders and turf, and thatched with bent and sea-ware; yellow gowans, green-grass, red thistles, and white flowers grew on the roof and waved in the wind, while the blue peat smoke curled up through a narel at the end of the roof. The fire was on the clay floor inside, and the smith's forge was at the end of the house. There Duncan had lived for many a long year, and there he was living with an old wife, an old mare, and an old dog for company. He had no son nor daughter, and never a man of his clan to bury him when his time should come.

2. When work was done in the smithy, or when there was no work to do, this old smith used to go out in the evening to fish in an old crazy boat; and many a time he had scanty fare, for fish are scarce and hard to catch in stormy weather in the west country.

3. On a day of these days, longer ago than you can remember, or than I can tell, he was fishing in the gloaming as he used to do, but he could catch nothing.

4. At last, just at the mouth of night, a mermaid rose at the side of his boat, and she said.

"Well, Duncan, are you getting fish?"

Now, as everyone in these parts knows full well, mermaids are sea-monsters, half-woman, half-fish, with long yellow hair which they comb when they sit on the rocks to bask. They are very fond of music, they are very rich, and they are able to do many wonderful things. They often endow men and women with magical powers, and sometimes they fall in love with land people and marry them. So Duncan the smith answered the mermaid as he would have answered one of his land friends.

"No," said he, "I'm getting no fish at all."

"What will you give me," said the mermaid, "if I send you plenty of fish."

"Well then," said he, "I have but little to give."

"What have you got at home?" said the mermaid.

"Well," said the fisher, "I have an old wife, and an old white mare, and an old black dog, and that is all the stock that I have in the world."

"Will you give me your first son when he is three years old?" said the mermaid, "if I send you fish."

"I'll do that," said the fisher; and he thought that was a good bargain, for he had no son to give. "It's a bargain," said the mermaid, and down she sank.

5. It was too late to fish any more that night, so the fisher sculled home and went to bed.

But if the sun rose early next day the fisher rose earlier than she did, and he went to the boat and out to sea, and there he fished his best. But all day long he caught nothing. At last in the time of dusk and lateness, what should he happen upon but a fish. He drew it up to the side of his boat, and reached out his hand to grasp it; but the fish with the hook in his throat opened his big mouth and gaped at him, and it gurgled and gasped out:

"Are you going to take me?"

"Well I am," said the fisher. "I'm glad enough to get even you."

"That's not the best thing for you to do," said the fish. "Let me go now and you shall have plenty of fish to-morrow."

So the old fisher pulled the hook out of the fish's throat and let him go, and home he rowed to his hut.

6. Home he went and dragged up his boat, and his wife met him.

"Well," said she, "have you got anything at all?"

"No," said he, "I have got nothing, but I shall get plenty to-morrow."

"What a pity it is that you came home empty to-night," said the wife.

"There's no help for it," said he.

And so they went supperless to bed.

7. Next morning he was up as early as the sun and off to sea to try his luck, but all day long he worked in vain. He could not catch hold of a fish, not a nibble could he get all day. But just at the mouth of night, at the time for coming home, the fish jerked and he struck and hauled up cheerily haul over haul. But when the fish came to the top it cried out:

"Are you going to take me with you to-night?"

"Well," said the old fisher, "I'm glad enough to have got you to take home."

"Oh," said the fish, rolling his eyes, "let me go to-night, it's best for you, and to-morrow you shall get something worth having."

So the fisher let the fish go, and home he rowed and dragged up his boat on the shingle, and shouldered his tackle, and walked up to his house door, and there his old wife met him again.

8. "Are you come home empty-handed again?" said she.

"I am, indeed," said the old man.

"Oh we shall not live," said the wife, we shall die." And so they went fasting to bed once more.

THE FISHER.

9. On the next day it was the same thing. The old man fished from sunrise to sundown, and never a bite got he till the time of dusk and lateness; and then in the mouth of the night, a fish laid on the hook. He hauled up cheerily, and when the head was by the side of the boat he gripped the fish fast by the throat.

"Are you going to take me?" said the fish.

"I am," said he, "I won't let you go any more."

"Well," said the fish, "it can't be helped. Have you any man to your clan?"

"No," said he, "I have in the whole wide world but my wife, my mare, and my dog."

Then the fish spoke once more and said:

"Thou shalt let no one split me, but do it thyself. Thou shalt put into the pot but a morsel of my liver and a bit of my heart to boil for thyself, and for thy wife, and for thy mare, and for thy dog to eat.

"Three bones thou wilt find at the side of my head. Go out and bury them in the garden.

"Thy wife will bear three sons.

"Thy mare will cast three foals.

"Thy dog will litter three whelps.

"When they are born dig up my bones and keep them.

"Three trees will sprout where the bones are buried, and they will be in leaf and budding, in sap and growing, summer and winter, spring and autumn, every day for ever, so long as the clan shall live.

"They will droop or wither or die as they do."

10. Home went the fisherman with the fish, and he did as he was bid. He split the fish himself, and he put a bit of the heart and a morsel of liver into the pot to boil, some for himself, some for his wife, some for his mare, some for his dog to eat; and when they had supped he buried the bones in the garden and went to bed and slept sound.

11. At the end of thrice three months the wife was brought to bed and she bore three sons.

"Oh my husband," said she, "what is here?"

"Three sons," said he.

"That were well," said she, "if there were aught to give them."

"That there is," said the old man.

Then he cast his eyes around, and the mare had cast three foals, and the hound had littered three whelps, and three trees had sprouted up in the garden. So he went out and dug up the bones and laid them aside as the fish had said.

12. "So time went on and the children grew, and the old man fished as usual, and he got plenty of fish. But as the third year came near its end he grew sorrowful and failed day by day. At the end of the third year, in the gloaming, the mermaid rose at the side of his boat and she said:

"Have you brought your eldest son?"

"No," said he. "I forgot that this was the day. I did not bring the lad."

"Well, well," said the mermaid, "you may keep him four years more to see if it be easier to part with him. See, here is his like for age. Is yours as fine as mine?" and she held up a big bouncing baby.

13. Home he went full of delight that he had four more years of his eldest son, and he kept on fishing and catching plenty of fish till the end of the second term was near. Then he grew sad and heavy, and failed daily. But when the end of the seven years had come he went to sea without his boy. The mermaid rose at the side of the boat and she said:—

"Have you brought me your eldest son?"

"Oh! I forgot him," said the old man.

"Go home," said the mermaid, "and keep your son for seven years more; but at the end of that time you will be sure to remember me. It will be no easier then to part with your son, but you shall have plenty of fish till then."

And down she dived into the deep sea.

14. So the old man cheered up and went home joyful, because he had got seven more years of his eldest son. He thought he would be dead before the term ended, and that he would never see the mermaid again. But time went on, and the end of fourteen years drew near, and the old man grew heavier and heavier, and weaker and weaker day by day, and his wife and his sons could not make out what ailed him.

"What is troubling you, father?" said the eldest son one day.

"The matter that does not concern thee touch it not," said the old fisher.

"But that which makes you sad concerns me," said the boy. "I must know what it is."

So the old fisher told his son how the whole matter stood between him and the mermaid, and how he was promised to the mermaid at the end of the fourteen years.

"Don't let that trouble you, father," said the boy. "I won't oppose you."

"No, my son," said he, "though I never get fish again for ever, I will not give you to the mermaid."

" Well, well," said the mermaid, " you may keep him four years more to see if it be easier to part with him. See, here is his like for age. Is yours as fine as mine ? " and she held up a big bouncing baby.

"Well, well," said the mermaid, "you may keep him four years more to see if it be easier to part with him. See, here is his like for age. is yours as fine as mine?" and she held up a big bouncing baby.

15. Now the sons had grown to great strength and wisdom, and the eldest son said to his father:

"If I may not go with you to sea any more, I will go out into the world to seek my fortune."

"That is but a poor prospect for me," said the old man. "It was long before I saw you, and it may be longer before I see you again. But if you must go you must not go empty. You must have a horse and a hound and a weapon to wield."

16. "A black horse was foaled when you were born. Here take this halter and this little rusty bit, and go out to the hill and shake the bridle, and the horse will come and put his nose into it.

17. "A black whelp was littered when the horse was foaled. Here take this cake and go out to the wood, and when the black hound comes baying openmouthed, give him the cake and he will follow you.

18. "I will go to the smithy and forge you a weapon myself."

19. Now this lad had grown so great and stout and strong, that his like was not to be found for size and strength and courage and goodly seeming, so he took the little rusty bit and the old ragged halter and strode up the hill to seek the black palfrey. He had not got far on the moor when the wild, shaggy, prancing, black palfrey came galloping down with clattering hoofs and shining eyes and streaming mane and snorting blood-red nostrils and open streaming mouth, rushing as if to trample the lad under foot and tear him; but the lad shook the bit till it clinked and rang, and the black steed came and put his nose into the halter, and they were good friends at once.

20. He took the halter in his hand and led the steed down to the forest. When they got there a great shaggy black hound came baying furiously out of the wood, with fiery eyes and blood-red tongue and glittering white savage teeth, glancing as if to seize and tear them. But the lad was not a bit afraid. He pulled out the little cake that his father had given him, and thrust it into the hound's open throat; and then the black dog was as tame as the black horse, and both followed the lad home to his father's hut.

THE WEAPON.

21. "And now, father," said he, "make me a weapon."

So the old smith went out to his smithy and weighed out iron enough to make a stout staff a stone weight, and he smithied it well while his son looked on. When it was done he took it and shook it, and it bent and broke in his grasp.

"That is not strong enough," said the lad, "for me. Let's make another."

22. So the old smith weighed out two stone of iron and they smithied a great iron club like the first. Then the lad took it and shook it, and it bent and broke like the first.

"That is far too weak," said the smith's son.

23. So the old smith weighed out three stone of iron, and they beat it and hammered and smithied, and forged a great bar; and when that was done he took it and shook it and it bent.

"That's too weak," said the lad, "if I were insulted."

24. So they weighed out four stone of iron, and forged a great bar; and when that was done the lad took it and shook it like a reed and it bent again. "That's not strong yet," he said, "if I were angry."

25. So they weighed out five stone and made another bar, and that bent like the rest.

"That would not serve if I were in a right good rage," said the lad.

26. So they weighed six stone of iron and smithied a great bent club like a shinny, and when that was made and cooled the smith's son said, "that will do."

27. Then he got up and went in to his house, and sought out the first of the fish bones which he buried, and dug up from the root of the first tree that sprouted on the night when his sons were born. He went back to the smithy and reached out his hand to his eldest son. "Here," said he, "take that and try it."

28. The lad took the little bone and gripped it and stretched out his arm and shook it, and the bone became a gold-hilted, glittering glaive in his grasp.

29. "Thanks to thee, Oh King of Princes and Mercies," said the lad. "Now I have done learning, wisdom, and knowledge, and now I may start. Yonder tree will be in bud, blossom, and leaf from autumn to summer, and from spring to winter, now and for ever till I meet death; and when I am dead the buds will fall off my tree."

30. The smith's sons would all three start and try their fortune; and each got his horse and hound and club and sword.[64]

31. They rose with the dawn and saddled their black steeds and called their black dogs, and hung their gleaming gold-hilted blades at their sides. They sought and got their mother's blessing.

"Son," said the old man to the eldest, "be sure that you never go within reach of the wind of the sea-shore."

"I will go," said he, "where there never was a drop of brine."

Then they left their blessings at home and set off to seek fortune; and so they took the world for their pillow and started on their way.

---

[64] In a Berneray version three sons start together.

THE THREE WAYS.

32. Thus this poor old man who lived long ago had three sons who thought that they would leave their father, and that they would go out into the world to seek their fortunes. The leash of lads set off together upon one way, and they kept going on till they reached a road that spread in three branches. They said to each other when they saw these three ways, that each should take a separate path, and that they should meet there in a year and a day, and so they did, and parted.

The eldest took the way that went east. The middle brother took the middle way. The youngest took the road that went west.

33. The eldest son rode east, away from the seashore and the smell of the brine, rode into the wood till the sun was high and he did not know where he was. He could see nothing but a wilderness of trees.

34. At last he came to an open space where he saw a wolf, a hawk, and a fox standing beside a year-old sheep.

"Stop," said the wolf, "and divide this carcase amongst us."

So the lad got off his black horse and pulled out the little rusty knife that he used to have in his father's boat to split fish, and he cut the sheep into three shares and threw them down before the creatures, and bade them choose.

That pleased them well.

Said the wolf: "When you are hard-pressed, remember me."

Said the hawk: "When you are in dire straits, remember me."

Said the fox: "When you are at the worst, think of me."

35. The beasts and the bird blessed the fisher's son, and he blessed them, and he mounted again and on he rode through the forest at speed. Each road was crooked, and each path was smooth for him and for his black horse and hound. They went so fast that they caught the swift March wind that blew before them, and the swift March wind that followed after could not catch them. And so they rode and ran through the forest and trees, till the bright clear white clouds of day were going away, and the dark, dim, dusky black clouds of night were coming on apace; and then they reached the palace gate of a great king's castle in a realm that is not of this realm at all.

FIRST WAY.

36. He thought that he could not lodge in so fine a house, and he looked out into the darkness and saw a little light afar off. But if it was far off he was soon there, and he knocked at a low door. It was the lowliest house of all the place and the house of the herd. He tied his horse outside and in he went.

"May I have leave to stay here to-night?" said he to the herd's wife. But she gave him no answer. Now that herd had no children. He did not know whether to go or stay, or where to go if he went away, so he stayed where he was.

Between then and a while the herd himself came home.

"Whose horse is that at my door?" said he.

"It's mine," said the lad.

"Wife, did you give the wayfarer food?" said the man.

"I gave him none," she said. "He never asked it."

"Then make ready a meal for him at once," said the herd.

So the churlish wife began to make ready, and the two men began their tales.

"What news from the big town?" said the wife.

"If there were news we know that you would know it," said the man, "but mayhap the stranger does not know our news. A dragon comes out of the sea every year, and every year he must have a maiden from our land to take away. The king has neither son nor daughter but the one daughter, and the lot has fallen on her this year. If he is not at the strand with his only daughter to give her to the dragon that comes out of the sea, the highest stone in his castle will be lowest and the lowest highest, and all the realm will be ravaged by the beast. He has gathered all the people of this realm together to see if he can find ever a man of any kind or condition to guard his girl and gain her and half the realm while the king lives, and all the realm when the king dies, and he has found no man to go to the strand but a cock-eyed, carrotty-headed cook who was carving meat within with a big knife."

37. "Well," said the lad, "you may need a herd and I am seeking service; will you take me and let me live here and earn my meat."

"Yes," said the herd. "I need a lad to mind the king's cattle, and you will serve my turn well enough. It was fortune herself that sent you here, for the herd that I had before left me last night."

The lad took service with the king's herd, and there he lodged.

38. In the morning the herd gave him charge of the cows, and he said: "Watch them well, but take good care that you do not let them into the closed park with the boarded gate; no herd ever put cattle into it that came alive out, and we should lose herd and herdsman."

"I'll take care of both," said the lad, and off he set wrapped in a gray garment.

39. There was an old brown cow that belonged to a widow and led the herd, and the herdsman followed with his horse and hound, but the pastures were bare.

40. So the herd went up to the park gate, and saw the finest grass he had ever seen. He opened the gate, and the brown cow led the cattle in, and there they stayed all day.

41. But as the evening drew on and milking time, he heard a noise. *Firum Farum*, little stones going under, *Firum Farum* great gravel going over, and he saw a great giant with seven heads and humps and seven necks coming

roaring down the park. He took three of the beasts by the tail and cast them on the very shower-top[65] of his shoulder and off he strode.

The herd thought it was better to suffer death than lose the beasts; so he ran to the park door and shut the gate.

"Mannikin, open the park gate," said the giant.

"I won't," said he.

42. Then the giant gripped the herd, and they fell to fighting with might and main. They made mire of rocks and rocks in mire; when least they sank they reached their knees, where most they sank they reached their eyes. At last the herd began to think he was far from friends and near his foes, and he thought of the wolf, and he was a wolf. And he gave the giant a little light easy lift and tossed him up and knocked him down and stood upon him.

43. "Death is upon you, giant," said the herd. "What's your *éric?*"[66]

"Oh, that's much," said the giant. "I have a copper castle and a copper whistle, and a ruddy russet-brown servant. I have a red dress, and a red horse that can fly through the air, meat and drink, and much treasure. Half to be yours while we live, and me to be your faithful comrade in good and evil: all to be yours when I die."

"That's mine and your life," said the herd. And he killed the giant.

44. Then he searched in the giant's pouch, and found the whistle and rode up to the copper castle and blew a blast. And the ruddy russet-brown servant came out, and he said:

"Well, now, I cannot but think that my master must be dead."

---

[65] Fras-mhullaich, G. H.

[66] *Éric* means the worth of a man; his ransom or the fee paid for man-slaying, the same as the blood-fine of Icelandic law.

"I'll be your master and not a whit worse," said the lad, and he asked for food and drink. That he got, and then he said:

"Don't let a pin's worth go hence till I come again."

"I won't, master," said the ruddy russet-brown servant who was in the copper castle.

45. The herd left the copper castle and gathered the skirt of his gray garment, and took the brown cow, and the rest followed him home. The old herd met him sauntering on, and he said:

"You have come back alive."

"Yes," said he.

"Did you see any man to harm or frighten you?"

"No," said he, "no one."

46. When the cattle were milked and all about the king's house were pleased—for they had not enough of milk-pails to hold the milk—they had to send for carpenters to make more—all the dairymaids and the old herd made much of the new herd, and gave him a good supper and lots to drink.

47. The lad lived with the herd, and every day he went to the grass park and the copper castle till the pasture grew bare. Then he thought he had better go further a-field, and he went in till he came to a second gate of boards and a second park, where the grass was as high as his knees. He opened the gate and let in the cows and there he stayed.

48. But he had not been there long when he heard a greater and a louder clatter than ever. *Firum, Farum*, little gravel going under; *Firum, Farum*, greater gravel going over; and he saw a big man coming. If no greater than the other he was no less, and he had seven heads and seven humps and seven throttles.

49. He came roaring into the park, and he seized six cows by the tails and slung them on to the shower-top of his shoulder and the ridge of his back.

50. The herd thought it better to suffer death than lose the cattle, so he ran to the gate of the park and shut it, and put his shoulder against it.

"Impudent elf, open the gate of my park," roared the giant. "I am not sure but that you may be the slayer of my brother, but I cannot think that such a mannikin did it."

51. He slung down the cows and sprang to the gate, and seized the lad with the gray garment; and then began a fight worse than the first. The lad was hard pressed; it seemed that he was near his foe and far from friends, and he thought once more of the wolf. Then he was a wolf, and he gave the giant a little gentle, cheery, easy lift, and he tossed him up and threw him down, and gave his heart and ribs a bump against the earth.

"Mine is your lying down and rising up, death is upon you," said the lad. "What's your *éric?*"

52. "That's much," said the giant. "I have a silver whistle and a silver castle, and a fine, fair, white servant in it. I have a white steed that can fly through air, or the sky; all is the same to her. I have a white dress, meat and drink, and much treasure; half to be yours while we live, all to be yours when I die, and I will be your faithful comrade and ally as long as I live."

"That's mine, and your death," said the lad.

Then he tucked up the tail of his gray garment and slew the giant.

53. Then he searched in the giant's pouch and found the silver whistle and rode to the silver castle and blew a shrill blast. Out came the fine, fair, white servant, and when he saw the herd he said:

"I do believe that my master must have died."

"I'll be master to you and no whit worse," said the lad; "quickly fetch me food and drink."

He got that, and then he said:

"Take care of all that is here till I come again."

"I'll do that, master," said the fine, fair, white servant that was in the silver castle.

54. Then the lad tucked up the tail of his gray garment, and took the brown cow, and the rest followed home.

55. The old herd met him and counted the cows and they were all there.

"Saw you anything to vex or frighten you?" said he.

"No," said the lad. "What should I see?" And he sauntered home.

"My best blessing will I give you," said the herd, "so safe as my cattle come home they never have come before."

56. And when the cattle came to be milked they had to send for more carpenters to make more milk-pails—such milk had never been seen in the king's dairy.

57. And all the maids made much of the herd, and gave him lots to eat and drink.

58. And the lad led the cows day by day to the park, and went to the silver castle and came home at night, and lived in the herd's house till the pasture began to fail.

59. One morning if the sun rose early he rose earlier still, and off he went to the third park far away. He opened the gate and went in, and found grass up to his waist, and there he laid himself out to bask in the sun.

60. But soon he heard a louder clatter than ever, rocks shaking, and stones flying; and a giant sprang into the park and seized more of the cows by the tail, and slung them on the shower-top of his shoulder and on the lofty ridge of his broad back. He had seven heads and seven humps and seven throttles like the others, and if he was no bigger than the other two, he certainly was no less.

61. Then the herd thought it were better to suffer death than lose the cattle, and he sprang up and shut the park gate and set his back to it.

"Open the gate, you insolent imp," said the giant. "Many a king's son and many a ritter have I cut heads off, and I will take off yours too."

"Two-thirds of your terror be on yourself and one-third on me. I know not why I should fear unless I must," said the lad.

62. Then the giant slung down the cows, and at each other they went till the herd fell on his knee.

"A king's son on his knee!" roared the giant. "He who went on his knee will go on his elbow."

Then the lad thought he was far from friends and near his foe, and he thought of his friends the beasts. And he was a wolf and a hawk and a fox all at once and turn about, and he was up and down, over and under, and all round the giant till he felled him and knocked the case of his heart and the side of his ribs bump against the hard earth.

"Death is upon you, giant," he said. "What's your *éric?*"

63. "That's much," said the old giant. "I have a golden whistle and a golden castle, a brave yellow-faced russet servant in the castle, a yellow palfrey that can fly through air or sky, a green dress, meat and drink, and much treasure: half to be yours while we live, all to be yours when I die, and I will be your faithful friend so long as I live."

"It's all mine, and your death to boot," said the lad, and he slew him.

64. Then the Gray Lad sought in the giant's pouch, and found the golden whistle. He gathered the skirts of his gray garment and shut the park gate, and up he went to the golden castle, and he played on the whistle and blew a blast, and the braw, yellow-faced russet servant came out of the castle, and said he:

"I really do think that my master must have died."

"I'll be your master," said the herd, "and no whit worse," and he got meat and drink.

"Keep all that is here for me till I come again." Then he went back and found the brown cow at the gate, and she led the herd home as before.

65. The herd met him, and counted the cows, and they were all there, and he said:

"Did you see anything to vex or frighten you to-day?"

"No," said the herd, "What should I see?"

And he sauntered home in his gray garment with the cows.

66. That night the carpenters had to send for more wood to make more pails for the milk; there was so much.

67. And the dairymaids were well pleased with the herd boy.

68. Next morning the herd went back to the park to see what he could find in the golden castle. He had not been long there when he saw a fearful great carlin coming, and she screamed out:

"You have killed my sons, and you have slain my husband, and now a draught of your blood shall quench my thirst."

She had a tooth for a staff and a tooth to stir the fire, and when she gaped, heart, liver, and lights could be seen through her open maw. The Gray Lad thought he had better flee, for so gruesome a carlin had never been seen.

69. He thought of the fox, and he thought of the hawk, and he was a hawk, and he flew to the top of the high tree.

"Come down till I eat you," said the carlin.

"Open your gab, then," said the herd, "till I jump down your throat."

70. The old carlin gaped wide, and the herd thrust his iron staff down her throat, and it came out at a mole in her breast, and down she fell.

Down jumped the herd upon her, and held her fast for fear she should get the staff out again. stomach g

"Death's upon you, carlin," said he, "what's your *éric?*"

78

"That's not little," said the carlin, "if so be that you get it."

71. "I have three great coffers: one under the foot-board full of gold and silver, two in the upper end of the castle full of all the wealth and wonderful treasure that man can think of.

72. "I have a golden comb. When used, there falls a golden shower from one side and a silver shower from the other. Whoso combs his hair with the coarse side is hideous, but whoso uses the fine side is handsome as man can be.

73. "I have a golden basin. Whoso washes in it becomes the most beautiful man on earth.

"I have a cloth[67] on which one can have any kind of meat.

"I have a cup[68] in which one can have any kind of drink.

74. "I have a glittering glass[69] dress.

"I have a pretty blue pacing palfrey that can fly through the sky.

"Though that's but little," said the lad, "it's mine, and your death," and he killed the carlin with his glittering steel blade.

75. Up he went to the castle and played upon the golden whistle, and the braw, yellow-russet servant came out.

He went into the golden castle, and found all the marvellous things that the carlin had.

He combed his head with the golden comb, and showers of gold and silver fell from his hair. He washed in the golden basin and put on the glittering glass garment, and never was seen so handsome a man since the world began. He ate and drank. Never did hungry herd taste such a meal. Then

---

[67] I. F. C. has scored these two out.

[68] I. F. C. has scored these two out.

[69] "Glass" is the translation, but anything that shines may be the meaning, say, polished armour.

when all was ended he laid his braveries bye, and gave them to his braw, yellow-russet servant to keep. He combed his head with the coarse side of the golden comb and he was shaggy and swarthy, sun-burnt, rough and scabby as he was before. He tucked up the skirts of his gray garment and went to the park gate, let out the brown cow, and sauntered home as usual.

THE MERMAID.

76. Then as usual the old herd met him and counted the cows, and said:

"Did anything happen to frighten you to-day? "No," said the herd, "nothing. What should happen?"

77. "I have news for you this day," said the herd.

"What's that?" said the Gray Lad.

The great "Biast" is coming out of the sea to take away the king's daughter, and unless he gets her the whole realm will be ravaged.

"I should care much more if evil befel our brown cow, than if it happens to the king's daughter," said the herd's boy; and home he sauntered to the herd's hut, and went to rest.

78. If the dawn came early next day, the herd rose earlier, and he took the cows and the brown cow at their head, and went straight to the first park. He opened the door of the park, and put them in, because there was no giant there now to meddle with or molest them. Then he tucked up the skirts of his gray garment, and up he went to the copper castle, and took out his copper whistle and played on it, and blew a shrill blast. The ruddy brown-russet servant came out and said:

"What's your will, master?"

"Meat and drink, horse and dress, arms and armour," said the lad.

That was ready, and when he had eaten and drunk his fill, he mounted and started.

81

79. Now when the king found that his only daughter had to be early out on the deep-dyed dark green hills, where the sun rises betimes and sets so late; and when he could find no man to guard her from the great sea monster that was to come out of the sea but the cock-eyed carrotty cook, who carved the meat with a great big knife in the king's kitchen, he sent them both off to the strand before sunrise, and fourteen full-armed, worthy warriors with them. When they got there, the king's daughter sat on a green mound by the seaside, and the cook went to the shore and flourished his carving-knife. He dug it into the sand and shouted:

"Though all the monsters in the sea, and all the warriors in Sorcha should come, thus will I do to them."

When he was tired he came to the king's daughter, and laid his head on her lap.

"Comb my hair," said he.

"Comb your filthy hair?" said the Princess, "you wretched scullion, not I."

80. Then they saw a shower coming from the West, and the sun in the East, and a glittering warrior with a flashing sword, with a ruddy russet dress, and a red horse riding swiftly from the eastern sky. And when they saw him, the fourteen full-armed worthy warriors fled to hide, and the cock-eyed carrotty-headed cook with the carving-knife ran away faster than they. And he hid in a dark hole where no man could see him and where he could see all.

81. Then the rider of the red palfrey came down to earth and tied his steed to the branch of a tree and came to the king's daughter, who sat sorrowful on the green mound by the deep-dyed dark green hills by the sea-shore, and he said:

"There's gloom on your face, girl; what ails you? and why are you here?"

"No matter," said she. "I shall not be here long, for the dragon is coming out of the sea for me, to take me away."

"I will stay with you," said the lad, "and keep you company for a while."

Then he laid his head in her lap to sleep and rest, and she combed his long hair.

82. "But if you sleep," said she, "what will rouse you?"

"If I sleep," said he, "nothing will rouse me but to cut off the tip of my left ear. Do that when the dragon comes."

And so they sat on the green mound in the morning sun, and the king's daughter combed the lad's long hair and he fell fast asleep.

83. He had not slept long when the lady looked and saw the dark squall coming from the West, the sea running East, and the waves waxing; and she tried to waken the lad. She laid his sword on his face and he stirred but slept on.

Then she saw the dragon coming in the squall with the rising tide and the waxing waves, spouting and blowing spray and spindrift from mouth and nose, and she was terribly frightened by the horrible noise of the fearful beast. She took the lad's bright sword and cut off the tip of his left ear, and up he rose and shook himself.

84. Then he shook a little rusty shaggy bridle that he had at his girdle and a black steed came and a black hound. He mounted the horse, and down to the strand he rode with the black hound at his heels.

85. And the dragon came to the strand, and he was so weighty that he sank in in the sand.

86. Then they fell upon each other with hard blows and much noise, rattling of stones, clashing of arms, baying and neighing, and shouting and roaring, splashing of billows and turmoil of wind and waves. Man and dog did the best they could, and the dragon fought as well; sometimes the dragon rolled over the man, sometimes the man rolled over the dragon.

87. At last the man thought that he was far from friends and near his foe, so he gathered his strength and clutched his sword and smote off one of the monster's heads.

88. "If I had a draught of fair water," said the dragon, "I would tear you to pieces now."

"If I had a draught of good red wine I would slay you this day," said the fisher's son.

89. "If one head is off two are on," said the dragon. "If the king's daughter is not here tomorrow at this same hour the realm shall be ravaged by me."

90. Then the dragon went back into the sea and went out of the loch with the ebb tide and the swelling waves of the ocean.

91. Then the lad picked up the dragon's head and tied it in a withy with a queer knot, and he sprang on his red horse and rode off to the eastern sky and disappeared.

92. Now the cook had hid in a place where no one could see him and where he could see every one, and when the coast was clear, out he came and seized the head and flourished his knife, and threatened the king's daughter with instant death if she dared to say that he did not do this deed of valour.

93. The fourteen full-armed worthy warriors of the king's guard when all was still came back, and found the cook with the dragon's head on a withy, and the king's daughter unharmed. They all marched back to the palace and boasted aloud.

94. But the king's daughter had the tip of the ear in her pocket.

95. The fisher's son went back to the copper castle and played on his copper whistle, and gave his red steed to be stabled by the ruddy russet-brown servant, and his dress to be laid aside. Meat he got and good red wine to drink, and when he had rested, he tucked up the skirts of his gray garment and went to the park and opened the gate, and let out the brown cow and the rest of the cattle, and sauntered home as was his wont.

96. "I have news for you to-day," said the old herd when he met him.

"What's that?" said the Gray Lad.

"The cock-eyed carrotty cook has cut one head off the beast that was to take away the king's daughter, but two heads are on yet, and they are to meet tomorrow."

"I had rather our brown cow were well than the realm and the king's girl," said the herd's boy.

97. "Well," said the herd. "It will be said of that cock-eyed cook: 'Many a good blade has a bad sheath.'"

"That's true enough," said the herd's boy, and home he went and slept in his dark crib.

98. If the day came soon, sooner than that the herd was up, and off he set with the cows to the second park. He went to the silver castle and sounded his silver whistle, and the fine fair servant came out and said: "What's your will, Master?"

"Meat and drink, horse and harness," said he.

That was ready, and when he had eaten and drunk he mounted and rode through the air.

99. The king's daughter, with the carrotty cockeyed cook and the fourteen fine, full-armed, worthy warriors were at the strand boasting and brandishing their blades as before.

100. But when the sun rose they looked to the East, and saw a gleaming, glittering warrior in silver armour riding through the air on a milk-white steed, with a gleaming, glancing sword of light in his right hand; and then they fled helter-skelter up to the deep dyed dark green hills, and the cook hid in his dark hole as he did before.

101. The rider of the milk-white steed came down to earth, and tied his horse to the branch of a tree and came to the king's daughter; and without more ado he laid his head in her lap, where she sat on the green knoll by the sea-shore, and there they talked for a time and a while, while she combed his hair.

102. "But," said she, "if you sleep how shall you be roused?"

"Lay my sword upon my face," he said, "and if that won't rouse me, cut off the tip of my little finger when the dragon comes."

103. Then he slept while the lady sat and combed his hair, and the cook looked out of the dark hole, where no one could see him and he could see all.

104. He had not slept long when the West grew dark with a coming squall, and the sea ran East and the waves waxed big and gurly, and the tide rose on the strand. Then she laid the bright steel on his face, and he stirred in his sleep but slept on.

Then she saw the dragon in the squall with the spindrift flying, blowing clouds of spray and steam from his mouth and throat and nostrils, and she seized the sword and shore off the tip of his right little finger, and up he rose.

105. He took from his girdle the little black rusty bit and the shaggy headstall and shook it—and the black steed and the black hound were at his side. He mounted, and to the strand he rode.

106. Then the dragon landed and trailed himself up, and he sank in the sand; he was so mighty and weighty, but this time he sank less, for he was lighter by one head.

107. "A hard fight for the king's daughter today," roared the dragon.

"A hard fight," shouted the herd boy, and at it they went. Horse and hound and man and monster rolled and roared, barked and bayed, and drove the sand and stones into the air, bit and fought and panted till they were tired. It was hard to say which had the best of the battle.

108. At last the herd thought that he was far from friend and too near a fearful foe, so he gathered his might and heaved up the beast, and he put his shoulder under and tossed him up and broke his ribs, and his shoulder-blade on the strand.

Then he grasped his shining steel sword and smote off a second head.

109. If I had a draught of water I would win yet," said the dragon.

"If I had a draught of good red wine I would slay you this day," said the herd.

110. One head is on if two are off," said the dragon. "I will be here to-morrow to take the king's daughter. If she is not here I'll ruin the realm."

111. Then the dragon trailed himself back to the sea, and went out with the ebb and the gurly waves of the dark west. Then the herd bound the head on a withy, mounted his white steed and went off swiftly.

112. Then out came the cock-eyed carrotty cook with his carving-knife, and danced and boasted and brandished his blade and took the head in his hand.

113. Then down came the worthy well-armed warriors of the king's guard, and they took the king's daughter home in triumph, and boasted and shouted more than ever they boasted before.

114. The herd went back to his silver castle and blew his whistle, and gave his milk-white steed and glittering silver armour to his fine fair servant to stable and keep; he called for meat and blood-red wine to drink, and when he had rested he donned his gray garment and gathered the skirts, and opened the park gate and let out the brown cow, and followed the beasts home as before.

115. "I've got right good news," said the old herd when he met the lad.

"What's that?" said he.

116. "It will be often said of that red-skulled cook that a good blade may have a bad sheath."

"What has he done now?" said the lad.

"He has brought home the dragon's second head and broken his ribs and his shoulder-blade, and the king's daughter is safe; and all the realm is rejoicing, for they hope to be rid of the dragon to-morrow."

"Is it so?" said the lad, and he went to the byre with the brown cow and the rest of them and went to bed.

117. Next morning long before dawn the herd was up and off to the third park with the cows. He put them in and went to his golden castle and played upon his golden whistle, and when the yellow russet servant came out, he said: "What's your will, master?"

"Meat and drink, horse and harness for a hard fight," said he.

That was ready, and when he had enough he mounted and rode west.

118. The king's daughter and all her company were at the same place. They looked East and they looked West, and they saw nothing but sky and sea.

119. Then the boasters began to brandish their weapons, and the carrotty, cock-eyed cook came to the king's daughter where she sat on the green knoll beside the sea-shore by the deep-dyed dark-green hills of Greece, and he laid his head on her lap.

120. Louse my head," said he. "You filthy scullion," said she. "Not I."

121. Then they looked West and they saw the squall, and they looked East and they saw the same. And they saw a rider riding through the sky in a glittering green garment on a yellow golden-brown palfrey, with a bright, glancing, glittering, bright sword of light in his right hand, and when they saw him they all fled to their lairs as was their wont.

122. The rider of the golden steed came down to earth and tied his horse to the branch and came to the king's daughter, and laid his hand on her lap at once.

123. "If I am hard pressed," he said, "give me a draught of wine."

"And where shall I get wine here?" said she.

"Take this golden cup," he said, "and give to me when I am hard pressed."

124. "And what will wake you if you sleep?" said she.

"Cut the size of a coin from the crown of my head," said he.

125. Then he laid his head in her lap, and she combed his long hair, and he slept for he was tired.

126. Then the tide began to rise, and the clouds to gather in the West, and the dark squall came down, and the sea ran East, and the waves waxed great and gurly green and blue and black. *The storm rose and the king's daughter quaked for fear, but the lad slept on.*

127. Then she saw the dragon coming up the loch with the spindrift flying, steaming and spouting, roaring and raving, and she took the sharp sword and shore a bit from the lad's scalp, a lock of his hair, and a bit of his skin, and up he rose and shook himself.

128. He shook his little black rusty bit and shaggy bridle-rein, and his black horse and hound were beside him.

129. The dragon landed where he landed before, and trailed himself up the sand, and sank in it, so vast and heavy he was; but he did not sink nearly so far, and he did not go so fast, for he was lighter and weaker.

130. The lad rode to meet him.

"A hard battle to-day," said the dragon.

"A stout fight," said the lad, and at it they went once more. Horse and hound, man and monster, neighing, baying, shouting and roaring, biting and fighting, struggling and wrestling, at hand grips they made little stones fly up, great rocks fall with the clatter of hard knocks. At last they were so tired that they stopped for breath.

131. "If I had a draught of water I would win yet and tear you to bits," said the dragon.

"If I had a draught of good wine I would slay you," said the herd.

"The storm rose and the king's daughter quaked for fear, but the lad slept on."

"The storm rose and the king's daughter quaked for fear, but the lad slept on."

90

" He cut off the dragon's third head, and won the fight."

He cut off the dragon's third head, and won the fight.

Then the king's daughter took wine and ran to the lad, and he drank a draught.[70]

---

[70] From a Gaelic version told by Dewar and Macnair. In Swedish, the princess aids by putting rags on the necks of the monster, for the heads when they touch water gain life and leap on again. This incident is in Gaelic also, and occurs at the end of this story.

132. Then he thought of the wolf and he was a wolf, and he tore at the dragon, and was a man and clutched his sword and cut off the dragon's third head, and won the fight.

133. And the dragon was a pool of water and a heap of sand.

Then he tied the head on a withy with a curious knot, and sprang on his golden steed and went the way he came.

134. Out came the cook and flourished his blade, and out came the well-armed worthy warriors of the king's guard, and home they went with the princess in triumph, for the dragon was dead and the cook had won the princess and half the realm; and when they got home, all the realm rejoiced that the dragon had died on the shore and would trouble them no further.

135. The lad rode back to his golden castle, and gave his green dress and his golden steed to the yellow-faced russet servant to tend and feed. When he was rested and feasted, he gathered the skirts of his gray garment and gathered his cows and followed them home.

136. The herd met him and said, "Good news to-night, my lad."

"What's that?" said he.

"The cook has killed the dragon and won the princess and half the realm, and all the people are bidden to a great wedding-feast that the king will give to-morrow. There is many a good blade in a bad sheath, and that cock-eyed carrotty cook is one."

"You don't say so," quoth the Gray Lad, and he sauntered home with his beasts, arid slept as if nothing had happened.

FIRST WAY.

137. Now the king's daughter and the carrotty cock-eyed cook were to have a hearty merry marriage-feast in the king's house, but the lad got up as usual and went off with the cows to the third park.[71]

138. He went to the golden castle and blew his whistle; when the yellow russet lad came out he said: "What's your will, master?"

That he told him, and when the time came he sauntered home as he used.

139. "Well," said the old herd, "I have more news."

"What's that?" said the lad.

The king's daughter says that she will marry no man unless he can loose the knots on the withies on which the dragon's heads are strung. The cook can't do it, and the fourteen fine, full-armed worthy warriors of the king's guard have tried all they can, and no man amongst them is able to loose the least of them. The king has bidden all the realm to the feast, and they are all feasting now.

"Why did you not go to the feast with the rest?" said the lad.

"I would not go and leave you alone," said the old herd.

---

[71] From the Fisher and the Gray Lad (with a bit inserted).

140. "What a well-decked wedding-board the king and his daughter have now," said the fisher's son. "I wish we had it here in front of us."

141. "Come here, my darling dog," said he, "and stretch your legs, and don't be lazy. Run to the bride's room, and fetch me the cloth that is spread on the board before the king and the bride and the carrotty cock-eyed cook."

142. Away ran the black dog, and up he went and in he stole to the bride's room. He seized the cloth and gathered it up before them all, and took it and ran to the herd's bothy and laid it on the board between them.

143. "Is there any one at all," said a counsellor that the king had, "who is not here? It is long since I heard it said: 'Strong is a whelp from a guiding breast.'[72] Send to the herds hut, and let us see if he is within or if any one is with him."

144. Away went three of the king's worthy warriors, and when they got to the herd's hut, there they found the herd and a stranger, and every bit that ought to be on the king's board spread on a cloth between.

Back they went as fast as they could, and told their tale.

145. "I said it once, and I say it now: 'A whelp is strong from a guiding breast,'" said the king's counsellor. "It was a pity to make such a grand wedding for that carrotty-headed cook who can't loose these knots. Go back and fetch the herd."

146. So the well-armed worthy warriors trotted back, and brought the herd, but he could not loose the knots any more than the rest.

147. "I said it before, and I say it once again," said the king's counsellor: "'A whelp is strong from a guiding breast.' Go down and fetch the herd's boy."

---

[72] Is làidir cuilean a uchd treòir.

148. So three worthy warriors went down to the herd's hut once more, and they said to the lad who sat there: "Who told you to take away all that was on the king's table? Come to the castle."

"I never took it, and I never stirred from here," said he, "and I don't mean to stir."

So the worthy warriors trotted back, and told their tale.

149. "Once more," said the counsellor, "I say that I have heard it said often: 'Strong is a whelp from a guiding breast.'"

"Get up you little band of worthy warriors from the king's guard, and go down and fetch up the herd's boy bound."

150. So the little band of warriors got up and marched down to the herd's hut where the boy sat with his black dog.

"Who told you to take all that ought to be on the king's board?" said they all. "You must come to the castle."

"I did not take the king's dinner," said the lad.

"If you did not take it, your dog did, and your dog is insolent," shouted all that little band of worthy warriors.

"Don't talk," said the captain, "but seize him and bind him, and take him as you were told."

151. "Arise, my puppy," said the fisher's son, "and haul them with the rhyme, and drag them against the rhyme, and out into the puddle at the door."

So the dog got up, and dragged them draggled through the puddle outside the herd's door and the byre.

152. Draggled as they were up went the little band to tell their tale, and the counsellor said: "I don't believe that that cock-eyed cook or the worthy warriors ever did that deed at all. Have I not said it: 'Strong is a whelp from a guiding breast'? Go down, you great band of fourteen well-armed worthy warriors of the king's guard and the bridegroom at your head, and fetch the herd's boy and his dog bound."

153. So the cock-eyed carrotty cook got his great carving knife, and the fourteen full-armed worthy warriors of the king's guard put on their martial array and marched to the herd's hut where the lad sat in his gray garment with his black dog.

154. "Why did you dare to take all that was on the king's board?" shouted all the great band.

"I did not," said the Gray Lad.

"If you did not your dog did, and he is insolent and ill-bred," said they all at once. "Why did you draggle the worthy warriors who came to fetch you?"

"I did not," said the fisher's son.

"Don't chatter with such a knave," said the bridegroom, "but bind him and bring him as you were bid."

155. "Arise my pup," said the herd's boy, "and seize them, and haul and pull and drag them, with the rhyme, and against the rhyme, and draggle them in the puddle that is outside."

156. So the black dog got up and drove and dragged and pulled and hauled the bridegroom with his bravery and his big knife and the fourteen full-armed worthy warriors of the king's great guard in all their martial array, with the rhyme and against, and up and down and out into the puddle that was at the door of the herd's byre outside.

157. When they got back all dirty and draggled the sage old counsellor said to the king: "Several times have I said that I have often heard it said, and I

say it again that it often will be said: 'A pup is strong from a guiding breast.' I don't believe that these draggled people slew the dragon."

158. "Come you," said the king to his gille, "and set in order the coach that we may send for the herd's boy."

159. So the coach was set in order, and sent to the herd's bothy where the lad sat with his black dog in his gray garment.

160. "Get up," said the gille, "the king wants you, and here is the coach come to fetch you."

161. So the lad got up and filled the coach with big stones and muck, and the gille had to go back.

162. Down came the king to see who was in his coach, and he opened the door. But if he did the stones and the muck tumbled out and nearly smothered him. I won't say what I have said," quoth the counsellor, but the best thing to be done now is to go yourself and fetch the herd's boy. So the coach was cleaned, and the king and the king's daughter and the counsellor got into it, and down they drove in state to the herd's hut.

163. When the Gray Lad saw that the king had come, he got up and got into the coach and drove to the king's castle. He got out and tucked up the skirts of his gray garment, and in he went to the room where all in the realm that were able to walk had been gathered, and there lay the dragon's three heads upon three withies, fastened with three knots which no one could loose.

164. So the swarthy, rough-skinned fisher's son, the herd's boy in his gray garment, walked up to the heads, and many who looked at the draggled-tailed gray garment sniggered and laughed and mocked him as he passed.

165. "Is there no one who can loose these knots?" said he.

Then he took the withies and loosed the knots one after the other, and the cook and the warriors began to quake.[73]

166. "Stop," said the king's daughter. "The man that slew the dragon and that I am to marry wants the tip of an ear, and the point of a finger, and a patch from the crown of his head. Sit still and quiet all that are set here about this chamber."

167. She went round the room from man to man, and all put out their hands and felt their ears and scratched their polls, but she never stopped till she got to the lad with the gray garment, who had his hand in his bosom.

168. "Put out your hand," said she.

"My hand is hurt," said he.

169. So the king's daughter snatched his hand and drew it out, and put her own into a pouch, and took out the tip of a little finger, and the tip of an ear, and a lock of hair with the skin of a scalp as big as a coin, and they all fitted.

170. "That's truth," said she. "It was you who slew the dragon, and you who rescued me, and I will never have any other to be bridegroom and lover. I am yours and half the realm while the king lives, and all the realm when he dies." And everybody shouted for joy except the cook.

171. The cook was hanged at once, and then the lad was to marry the king's daughter.

172. But he asked for two hours' grace, and that he got. Out he went and shook his rusty bridle, and the black steed came. He mounted and rode to the golden castle and blew the whistle, and when the yellow-faced russet lad came out, he said, "What's your will, master?"

---

[73] In another version, he loosens three sons of the King of Sorcha (light) whom he had conquered and bound.

173. "The best horse and the best dress in the castle," said the Gray Lad. That he got: the sky-blue pacing palfrey that could fly through the sky, and the glittering glass dress that the carlin had. He combed his hair with the golden comb till gold and silver showered from either side. He washed in the golden basin, and combed his locks with the fine side of the golden comb, and then he was the most beautiful man that the world had seen.

174. When he was thus arrayed, he mounted and rode through the air to the king's castle, and the king's daughter came out to meet him. They went to the castle hall. A churchman was got, and they were married.

175. A great and wonderful wedding was made for them, and they sent me home and gave me neither welcome nor guest-room there.

176. Now, after the fisher's first son had been married for some time to the king's daughter, it so fell out that she longed greatly for dulse,[74] and she asked the lad to go with her to the strand to seek it. The lad forgot his promise to his father, and they took their way to the sea-shore, where the brown sea-ware was rising and sinking amongst the blue waves, below the deep-dyed dark-green hills of Greece.

But while they were straying and playing and gathering dulse amongst reefs and stones on the ebb, the mermaid rose and made a rush, and seized the lad and shouted:

"It is many a day since you were promised to me, and now I have you perforce," and then she swallowed him up alive.

177. The bride, when she saw what had happened, fled to shore, weeping and wailing in shadow and darkness, sad and tearful and sorrowful for the loss of her married mate. She sat by the shore wringing her hands till the tide rose, and then she went back to the castle where the counsellor was, to ask his aid.

---

[74] A fucus which grows upon rocks and upon other sea-ware, and comes above water at low tide. It is good to eat, and tastes somewhat like nuts and sea-water.

178. What shall I do?" said she. "What shall I do? For a mermaid has taken away my married man, and I am left alone. How shall I find a way to get my man back?"

"This do," said the counsellor. "Go down with all the dresses and braveries and jewellery that you have, and spread them out by the sea-shore. Take your harp and play."

And much more he said which she did, and I omit in order to avoid telling the story many times as reciters always do when they spin yarns.

" She sat on a green mound in the gloaming in the mouth of the evening, playing on her harp."

"She sat on a green mound in the gloaming in the mouth of the evening, playing on her harp."

179. Down she went with all that she held most precious—dresses and jewels and things of price—and she spread them on the rocks by the sea. She sat on a green mound in the gloaming in the mouth of the evening, playing on her harp beside them.

180. She had not sat long there playing in the dark when the mermaid rose outside the surf, for mermaids are fonder of music than any other creatures, and there she floated, listening; but when the king's daughter saw the mermaid, she stopped.

181. "Play on," said the mermaid.

"No," said she, "not till I see my man again."

So the mermaid opened her great mouth and gaped, and showed the lad's head, and the king's daughter knew that he was alive.

182. "What fine things you have there!" said the mermaid, as she swam close to the shore.

"Yes," said she. "I would give them for my husband."

"Well, then, play on," said the mermaid.

183. So the lady sat on the green mound and played, and the mermaid lay in the brown sea-ware and listened, and opened her mouth and gaped, and showed the lad to the waist, and swallowed him down again.

184. Then the lady stopped, and the mermaid said again:

"What fine things you have there on the rocks!"

"Yes," said she, "I would give them all for my husband."

"Well, then, play on," said the mermaid.

185. So the lady played on, and the mermaid rolled amongst the brown sea-ware in the blue water amongst the waves, and she opened her mouth once more and took out the lad altogether, and placed him upon her open palm.

186. But he, when he was free, thought of the falcon, and was a falcon, and flew and darted to shore, and was free.

187. But when the mermaid saw that her prey was gone,, she made a snatch at the wife and took her away instead.

188. When the lad saw that the mermaid had taken away his wife, he was wild with grief, and mad with rage, and did not know what to do, so he went to the counsellor and asked his aid.

189. "Well," said the counsellor, "there is but one way to win your wife, and that is to take the mermaid's life."

"And how is that to be done?" said the lad.

"The mermaid's life," said the counsellor, "is not in her, and it is easy to take. It is in an egg, which is in a fish, which is in a duck, which is in a ram, which is in a wood, under a house on an island, in a lake."

190. Now the lad thought that the first thing to be done was to get to the loch. So he went to his golden castle and donned his glittering glass dress, and mounted the sky-blue palfrey, and took his gold-hilted glaive of light in his hand, and his dress became him well.

191. He rode and rode till he reached the loch, and then at a bound the horse was in the island.

192. He found the house in a wood, and he dug under the stance, and found a flag-stone.

193. He raised it and out rushed a ram.

194. So he thought of the wolf, and was a wolf, and he chased the ram all round the island, and caught and slew it.

195. But when the ram was slain and torn open, a duck flapped out of his inside, and flew swiftly off to the sky.

196. Then he thought of the falcon, and was a falcon, and flew a swift flight till he soared over the loch above the duck, and then he stooped and struck.

197. But as he did, a fish fell from the duck out into the loch, and the falcon flew to shore, and was a man.

198. But the lad could not think what to do next.

199. So he thought of the fox, and was a fox, and he found out an otter's den on the island, and seized the cubs.[75]

200. "Let go my cubs," said the otter to the fox, "and I will be your faithful ally for ever."

"Well, then," said the fox, "fetch me the fish that fell in the loch from the duck just now."

201. So the otter dived out into the water like an oiled stick, and rose quickly with a trout.

202. But out of the trout's mouth rolled an egg, and the lad seized it, and set his foot on it amongst the stones on the shore.

203. Then the mermaid rose in the loch, and roared a roar, and screamed a yell, and cried out: "Break not the egg, and you shall have all you ask."

204. "Give back my wife," said the lad. So the mermaid swam to shore and opened her mouth, and the wife sprang on dry land, safe and sound.

---

[75] As Donald Macphie related

205. When he got her hand in his, he crushed the egg with his foot against the stones, and the mermaid was a heap on the rocks.

206. There was joy and delight in the king's castle that night, for the king's daughter was safe, and the dragon was slain, and the mermaid dead, and when the lad told how he had slain the great carlin, and the three big giants with their five heads and five humps and five throttles apiece, and how he had saved the king's cattle, and gained three castles, then the king gave him great honour and half his realm, and he was a mighty man with the monarch from that day forth, and, as they say in the Highlands, there I left them, but only to come back to them after awhile.

THE SECOND WAY.

207. Now, when the fisher's three sons parted at the three ways, the middle brother took the middle road with his black horse and his black dog, and his gold-hilted glaive by his side, and he rode up a steep hill.

208. He took the hill way, and when he got to the top of the mountains he fell in with a great plain, and on he went till he came to a place where a lion, a pigeon, and a rat were all three quarrelling over a grain of corn. He was not much afraid of them, and went to see the sight.

"Come hither, lad," said the lion, "and give just judgment between us three. You will be the better for it if you do, but if you give unjust judgment you shall be put to death."

"What think you of my being here?"

"Well," said he, "I have no very sure notion, but I think that you ought rather to be about the banks of rivers."

Then the pigeon said: "And what think you of my being in this place?"

"I'm not sure what to think," said he, "but I have a notion that you ought rather to be amongst boughs and banks and rocks," said he.

"And what think you of my being in such a place?" said the rat.

"I don't surely know," said the lad, "but I am sure of this, that you ought to be gathering a shelter to keep ready for winter."

That pleased them well. Then the lad thought awhile, and spoke.

105

"You, lion," he said, "I wonder that you who have been raised above all the beasts of the field, should think it worth while to quarrel with a rat about a grain of barley. And you, pigeon, who can fly so far and fast through the sky, and gather so much, I wonder that you should dispute one grain of corn with a rat."

Then the lion spoke for the rest, and he said—

"Well hast thou judged. The rat has best right to the barley-corn. We three were put under spells here to remain as lion, pigeon, and rat, and we were to dispute about this barley-corn till some one should come to give us right. Because of my might all that came before judged that I had the right, and I slew them all. We are kings altogether, and you have done us great service. Each of us will be a king again, and may go to his own realm, and for your help to me your reward shall be that whenever you think of me, you may be a lion, so that you may do a lion's exploits."

Then the pigeon said: "You have done me great service, and my gift is: If ever you need it, you need but to think of me and you will be in this form."

Said the rat: "He has done me as great a service as to either of you, and whenever he thinks of me he may be a rat, and though I be the sorriest amongst you, it may well be that it will serve him as well to be a rat as to be in the shape of either of you."

They went away, and he never asked what realm belonged to any one of them.

209. On he went and on he rode as swiftly as ever his brother did, till he came to a realm that he did not know. To all whom he met he spoke, and asked his road. All who knew it, answered. All who did not, gave him a civil reply, and so he went, and hurried till the evening was coming on, and he saw a great house before him, and a big town, and they told him it was the house of the king.

210. So when he saw the king's castle, he came to the gate as a poor lad seeking service. He told his errand at the gate, and word was sent in to the king that a sturdy lad was at the gate seeking service. He was sent for, and it was settled that he should serve in the kitchen under the hand of the great

cook, and he was called the little cook, and he was the best servant that the king ever had.

211. He was there awhile, and he never saw a woman at all in the place. So one day he asked the head cook if there was ever a woman there at all.

"There is no woman here at all," said the head cook, "but the king's daughter, and it is not everyone who can get to her room."

"And where may that room be?" said the cook's mate.

"It is at the northern end," said the cook, "in a tower."

212. Now one day it so fell out that the king had an errand, and the lad had to go to a house that was far away. The king wanted to give him a horse, but he said:

213. "I would rather be without a horse, for I am not used to horses. But if you send a man on horseback I will be back before him."

That the king would not credit, but he thought that he would try. So a horseman was sent, and the little cook set off horseless to see who could soonest get back with the king's errand.

214. No sooner was the lad out of sight of the castle than he thought of the pigeon, and he was a pigeon, and flew to the journey's end and got the matter, and he was back before the horseman had got half-way there. The king would not believe that he had been there at all, till the rider returned.

215. "And where is the thing that I sent you to fetch?" said the king.

"They told me that the cook's mate got there before I did, and fetched it," said the rider.

The king was amazed, and he was very fond of the lad after that.

216. Nevertheless, he had to sleep in the kitchen with a hound, and his company did not displease him, for he knew that she would tell no tales.

217. Now it so happened that the cook's mate on his errands about the house saw the king's daughter, and spoke to her; and one night he thought that he

would pay her a visit in her chamber. So he threw a somersault out of heel and became a pigeon, and flew out of the window to the northern end of the castle, and to the top of the chimney, and down on to the floor, and then he was himself again in a trice.

218. The king's daughter was sleeping sound, so he crept to the bedside and tried to steal a ring off her finger.

219. But the king's daughter awoke in a fright and cried out, and all the guards and sentries and the king himself came rushing to help her.

220. But before they got the door open, he thought of the rat, and was a rat, and fled under the bed and hid in an old bacholl of a shoe.

221. The king and all his guard came clattering in and cried together: "What is the matter?"

222. "Oh!" said the king's daughter, "there is a man in the room. He came to my bedside and tried to steal the ring off my finger, but I awoke and cried out."

223. The guards searched and the king sought, and they kicked the old shoe hither and thither, but the little lad lay hid, and they found no one. When they were tired the king said:

"There is nobody in the room."

"Somebody was in this room when I called out," said she.

So the king and the guards sought again to see if there was any way to get out when the door was locked, and they peeped up the chimney and everywhere else, and there was no place to get out of the room but the room door.

224. So the king flew in great rage, and he growled: "Daughter, if you ever dare to make such a disturbance and rout about the house again, I will give it to you with my sword when I come up."

So he marched out and locked the door behind him.

225. When they were all gone, the lad came out of the old shoe and turned heels over head, and was a lad again, and he seized her hand and stole the ring.

226. But since she did not dare to cry out for fear of the king, she said softly

"Where were you when they were searching the room?"

"I was in the room all the time," said he.

"And who are you?" said she.

"I am your father's head-cook," said he.

"That you are not," said she, "but I should like to know who you are. But since you can come here, if you come again I will give you a gift, for such is the custom in this country." Away he went as he came, and back to his kennel beside the dog who could tell no tales.

227. After a few days the lad thought that he would go the same way to see what might happen, and before he went away from the room the lady gave him a waistcoat (*peiteag*) embroidered with needlework, and told him to go with it to the fair at the big town next day.

228. He was a pigeon, and up the chimney and in at the kitchen window, and into his kennel in a trice, but the waistcoat he stowed in his box.

229. Next morning the head-cook was making himself smart for the fair, so the cook's mate began to wash his face.

"Are you going any way?" said the cook.

"I am going to the fair," said the other.

"You must not go," said the head-cook, "I am going."

The lad said never a word, but he opened his box, and took out the waistcoat and put it on.

"Wherever did you get such a brave (*briagh*) waistcoat?" said the great cook.

"No matter where, I have it," said the lad.

"I'd give you a good price for it to go to the fair in, if you would give it to me," said the great cook.

230. "Well," said the other, "I won't be hard upon you. If you will give me seven bellyfuls before we go, and seven bellyfuls when we come back, you shall have the waistcoat for the fair."

So the lad got lots to eat, and the cook got the waistcoat, and put it on and went to the fair.

231. When he was there, the king's daughter came to look if she could see who wore the waistcoat, but when she saw the cook with the waistcoat on, her hands fell down by her sides, and she went home.

232. When the cook came home, his mate met him. "Well," said he, "did you see the king's daughter at the fair?"

"Yes," said he, "I saw her."

"Did she speak to you?" said the lad.

"She did not speak," said the great cook, "but as soon as ever she saw me she turned home."

" She is in love with you," said the lad.

"That is exactly what I supposed," said the king's head-cook.

233. That night, when everybody else went to bed, the cook's mate and the dog went to their kennel, but they had not been there long when the lad turned heels over head and was a pigeon, and out of the window and up in the chimney, and down on the floor of the north room, and there he stood as a handsome lad in the lady's room.

234. "Why were you not at the fair?" said she.

"Was I not?" said he.

"No," said she. "And I wish you would tell me who you are."

"Am I not your father's head-cook?" said he.

Not you," said she, and this time she gave him a pair of garters and bade him wear them at the fair for her sake.

Back he went, and these he stowed in his box as before.

235. Next morning it was the same story as last day. The cook put on a pair of short breeks, as was the fashion of Frenchmen in these days,[76] and the cook's mate cleaned himself and produced his grand garters. Such garters the head-cook had never seen, and he got a loan of them for the same price seven good bellyfuls before he went to the fair and seven more when he came back.

236. He put on the garters and went. But when the king's daughter saw the cook arrayed in the broidered waistcoat and the grand gay garters, her arms drooped, and she had to go home for fear she should faint.

237. "Did you see the princess at the fair?" said the lad, when he came home, "and did she speak to you to-day?"

"I saw her," said the head-cook, "and she saw me, and as soon as ever she did her arms fell by her sides, and she went home."

"She must be in love with you," said the cook's mate.

"I rather think that she is," said the king's head-cook.

238. That night it was the same story. The lad went to see the princess, and before he went away she gave him a cap (*biorraid*) to put on his head, and bade him wear it at the fair, for it was the fashion in that country for ladies to give keepsakes to lads whom they liked.

239. Next morning it was the same thing again. The head-cook got a loan of the grand cap, and the little cook stayed at home and had plenty to eat. But when the princess saw the cook with the grand gay garters and the broidered vest and the biorraid on his head as grand as a lord, she nearly fainted, and home she went as fast as she could.

---

[76] According to Macnair.

240. When the cook got home and told his tale, his mate was sure that the princess had fallen in love with him; and he rather thought that that was the case.

241. A while after that there came a herald (*teachdaire*) from the Turkish emperor,[77] or from another powerful king.[78] He came to seek the king's daughter, and if she were not given at once, the Turkish emperor was to come to fight him. The king gathered the nobles of the realm[79] to get counsel from them, and he said:

"Daughter, I think it will be best to give you, for I have not got men enough to fight the Turks. It will be best to send word to the emperor that you will go."

242. "It will be cast up to me afterwards," said she, "if it is said that the realm of France could not hold one day's battle."

The high counsellors were gathered, and the king put the question before them whether war or submission to the Turks was best, and the counsel that they made out at last was that war was better than too easy submission. So the king sent a herald to the Turkish emperor to say that he would not give up his daughter in spite of him. It was to be battle.

243. The king gathered all his people,—head-cook, little cook, and all—and he set out to meet the Turks.

244. But when he was near the field of battle, they remembered that they had left their standard behind. They could do no good without the flag, and there was but little time to fetch it. The flag was in the bedroom of the king's daughter, at the top of the castle, at the north end; and there was the king's armour[80] too, hung up at the bedside, as men in the isles hang their garments on a peg, for that too was forgotten.

---

[77] According to Macnair.

[78] According to an island authority who has less history.

[79] *Maithean na rioghachd.*

[80] *Deise chruadhach.*

245. Now, if the king had these he thought that he might win the battle.[81]

246. "Oh," said the king, "is there any one in the camp who will try to bring the flag and my armour before the battle begins? If I gain, he shall have my daughter for reward, and my realm when I die, but if he fails his head shall be cut off at once."

247. There was no one who would leave the field but the head-cook, and off he set in great haste homewards.

248. But the cook's mate took a turn aside and turned head over heels, and was a pigeon, and flew his best flight to the castle, and was a man, and ran upstairs and he shouted to the king's daughter—

249. "Open quickly, for there is great haste and need of the standard."

"I know your voice," said she. "I need not open the door, you have a way of opening it; come in as you came before."

"I have no way of opening doors," said he.

"Whether or no," said she, "you have some way to come into this chamber, so enter."

250. When he saw that there was no help for it, he turned over, and was a pigeon, and out of the window and up and down the chimney, and there stood before her the handsome lad that came to seek service at her father's castle, and not the head-cook.

"I see who you are now, lad," said she, "and how you got in, but where were you when they sought you."

251. "I was in yonder old bacholl of a shoe," said he; and he turned heels over head, and was a rat, and into the shoe and out again and himself in a trice.

---

[81] Probably because Macleod's fairy flag and ancient Norse standards are, and were, supposed to be magical.

252. "No one who could do all these tricks but could do a third," said the princess. "Show me another trick."

"I am afraid you will be frightened," said he.

"I won't be frightened for you in any shape of seeming," said she.

So he turned over and was a great lion.

253. But she took her shears, and shore a lock from his shaggy beard, and kept it, and she gave him the flag and armour.

254. Then he took another turn and was a pigeon, and flew till he met the head-cook coming at about a third of the way back.

255. He met him and gave him the flag and armour, and he was back at the camp in time.

256. Then the fight began. The king put his soldiers in order of battle, and the Turks went to meet them, and victory was with the Turks.

257. The French were fleeing at each place in the field. So the little cook's mate stole into a thicket, and thought of the lion, and he was a lion himself.

And, as the old lady in Berneray says, what should he do but turn back all and whole of the king's foes. He tore and smashed and killed everyone, and drove the field with the king. According to Macnair, he also showed generalship, for he began at the Turks at the end that was farthest off, and put them out of order of battle. The French rallied, and the rout was on the Turks at the last. They fled to their ships, and very few escaped alive on board.[82]

Then the head-cook, like Raja Vivata, said that he had gained the fight, and he it was who brought the flag and the king's mail, and so he was to have the princess, and be heir to the realm.

---

[82] Which is a fair description of a Scandinavian battle in which sea-rovers got the worst of the fight. Be that as it may, the story remains in its own shape, and it is rather like the Exploit of Bhima in the Mahabharata, who won a battle single-handed.

258. The whole array marched back in triumph, and matters were set in order for a grand wedding.

259. The nobles were asked, and all the realm was gathered, and the cook sat at the end of the board, at the high end, exceedingly proud. Drinking and music and joy were up, and word was sent for a priest, so that the wedding knot might be tied.

260. The priest came, and the cook was in great haste to get it all over, for he was very tired and sleepy.

261. Then the king's daughter stood up and said: "There is one who ought to be here, and is not."

"All the household are here but the cook's mate," said the Grand Kitchener, "and it does not signify whether he is here or not."

"No one of the household is to be absent from my wedding," said she.

262. So a messenger was sent for him, but he would not come.

263. Then another and more honourable messenger was sent, and he would not come.

264. Then the bride herself went down to the kitchen where the lad was.

"And why did you not come to be at my wedding?" said she.

265. "I never was asked," said he, as his brother said in the like case.

"You were asked," said she.

"You did not ask me," said he.

266. Then she grasped his hand and said: "Come up with me, then." And so he went.

When she got to the guests, she said:

"Here is one who can turn twists and play tricks that will cause you wonder. Do one for me," she said to the lad.

"Perhaps you will be frightened," said he.

"No," they said that they would not.

267. So the lad turned over and was a rat, and he ran about the floor, and nibbled the ladies' feet till they screamed and yelled and laughed.

268. Then he turned over again and was a pigeon, and flew, and stood on the ladies' knees, and all were pleased, and stroked his feathers till they were like to hurt him; they were so pleased with the pretty bird.

269. But when he had been all round the company, he flew up to the lights and flapped them out with his wings, and then the ladies giggled and laughed, and said that they had never before seen a man turn himself into a rat and a pigeon in this strange fashion.

270. Then all begged that he would play another trick, and when the lights were lit once more, he gave another turn, and was a lion, gaping and roaring all about the room, and the ladies fled and tumbled about for fear, as did the Grand Kitchener, and all but the king and his daughter.

271. "Aha," said the king. "This is the man who did the deeds this day, and not me."

272. Then the princess fitted the yellow lock in the lion's shaggy beard, and she told that this was the man who fetched the flag, and that she had seen him play all the tricks.

273. Then the lion turned over, and was a very handsome lad, as likely to look upon as any in the whole realm, and all allowed that such a lad ought to have the princess.

274. So the cook's mate was married to the daughter of the French king, and the herd's boy was married to the daughter of the King of Greece, and the Lord High Grand Kitchener was sad, and disagreed, and left the company.

275. That wedding lasted for six days of the week, with drink, and music, and great rejoicing, and there I left the fisher's second son at the end of the second way.

276. The third brother, when he parted from the others, rode west, as it is said in Berneray, where all ways would lead to the sea after a couple of miles, and he came to a great forest.

277. Up he went into the forest, to try if he could see houses or find any people of the place, but nothing could he see but a tangled wilderness of wood and birds and fruits that he had never seen before. At last, day was going, and night was coming.

278. He thought that it would be well if he could find some place or other where he might stay in the night, for he was afraid wild beasts of this forest might come *through the night* and slay him, and so he went wandering on, thinking that he should like to find a place where he might be safe in the night.

279. As he went, he saw a great castle before him, with a rampart wall about it. At first he feared to go on, for he did not know whether peaceful people or fierce men were within, or whether they might not slay him. But spite of danger, he risked going on.

280. He reached the castle, and he saw no one at all. He went round about the rampart till he came to a gate, and he went in by the gate, and looked all round, and still he saw no one.

281. He saw an open door in the castle, and he went in, but still he saw nobody there.

282. He went in past other two doors, and into a room where there was a fire.

283. He sat at the fireside, and there he stayed for awhile waiting, but he saw none living.[83]

284. But a candle and a candlestick came into the room where he sat, and the candle and candlestick stood upon the board, and the candle gave light through the chambers.

---

[83] *Gin*, lit., any begotten being; creature.

285. When he had sat for a long time and saw no one, he began to be tired of waiting, and to long.

286. He thought that food might do him good if he could get it.

In an instant the board was spread, and his choice of every food that was better than another was on it. He sat a while staring at the board, but still he saw no one living; and he was very hungry. At last he thought that he might as well eat part of the food, whatever the matter might mean; so he sat by the side of the table, and he ate till he had enough. Then he sat at the fireside again.

287. When he had sat awhile by the fire, he began to grow sleepy.

Then it seemed to him that if he had a bed he would go to rest.

288. The candle and the candlestick that stood upon the board went to the first door that was next to him, and the candlestick with the candle in it, stood at the door. He sat awhile looking at them, wondering at all he saw, but in time he took courage, and got up and went where they were.

289. They went when he came, till they came to another door, and there they stood.

290. It seemed to him that he might as well follow to see where they should go. On they went, till they got to the next door, and again he followed.

291. The third door was opened, and in he went to a wondrously gorgeous[84] chamber with a bed in it, and the bedclothes were choice and ready for going to bed. He stood awhile looking about him and looking at the bed, and at last he came to think that as he could see no one, he might as well go to bed. So he stripped off his clothes, and he lay down in the bed, and put the clothes over his head and slept.

292. The first time he awoke during the night, he seemed to perceive something like a human creature near him. This did not please him very well, so he moved from it as best he might, and he slept again. The next time he awoke it was day, and no one living was near him.

---

[84] *Anabharra riomhach.*

293. He looked about him, as he usually did. The chamber was very richly set in order. He lay awhile staring about, and at last he got up to put on his clothes. But when he looked, there was not a rag of his there. He sought backwards and forwards, and all about, but he had no clothes to find. But there was a dress of other clothes, and clothes that were very grand, lying just where he had laid his own. Since he could not find his own, he put on the clothes he found instead, and he went to the chamber where the fire was—the first in which he sat when he came to the castle over night. He found it with board decked and spread with each meat and drink that was best, so he sat and ate his fill.

294. When he had finished he looked about, and there he saw every sort of sporting gear[85] that he ever had seen, and many sorts that he never had seen before. He took what he understood the use of, and he went out to shoot in the forest, and that day he killed a couple of turkeys—which feat the old sailor or one of his messmates may have performed in America. These he took to the castle and cast on the ground, and when dinner-time came, one of them was ready. He wandered about the castle till "the night came," and when "the night came" he went in to the castle and to the chamber, where he was the night before, and he sat at the fireside.

295. Then came the candle and gave him light.

296. When he wished for supper, the board was decked. When he was sleepy, the candle led him from door to door, and he followed her, and went to bed and slept.

297. The first time he woke, he felt as though a human creature lay on the bed, but he said never a word and slept, and the next time he awoke "the day was there," and there was no one with him in the bed but himself.

298. He got up and found other and grander garments, and this time he was not so loath to put them on as he was the day before.

299. He went to the quarter where he was used to find food, and the fire was lit and the board decked, and when he had eaten, he went out to sport, and that day he killed two hares. These he took to the castle and cast on the

---

[85] *Inneal scilg.*

floor. One he found ready for dinner, and when the night came the candlestick with the candle in it came and stood upon the board, and the candle gave him light.

300. When he wished for supper, the supper was ready upon the table, and when he had eaten and wished to go to bed, the candle went before to show him the way, and he followed and lay down.

301. But he thought if anything should come near him, as on the other two nights, that he would speak, happen what might.

302. When he woke, he felt as though a human creature were near him, and he said:

"Who are you? and where am I?"

The thing that was near him said:

"I am the daughter of the king of the golden castle, and this is the castle. Here you may be well off if you will beware of yourself, and do that which is right, as you ought."

"If I knew what I ought to do I would do it," said he.

"What you ought to do," said she, "is to respect me, I am the candle and candlestick that you saw. I was laid under spells to be a candlestick with a lighted candle in it, till I should find some one to stay with me, and lay no hand upon me to touch me, till the end of a year and a day, as you are now doing. Then I shall be free of the spells, and you shall marry me, and have half the realm while my father lives, and the whole realm of the golden castle when he dies."

"If I may get that," said he, "I will stay here with you for a year and a day, if I get what I need in the meantime."

"You shall have all you desire," said she, "a suit of new clothes every day when you get up, your wish and choice of food, sporting gear and sport when you desire it, leave to go out and in as you see fit, but you will not see the face of man or woman here till my time of freedom comes. I am the candle that gives you light, you may look at me, here you may be when you wish to sleep, and here I will visit you, and talk with you, but touch me not. You will never know when I come or go. If you will live thus for a year and a day with me, you will do me great service, and serve yourself."

"I will do all you say," said the fisher's son. "I will make myself happy here, till you are freed from spells," and soon after he fell asleep.

303. When he awoke she was gone. All that day, and from day to day he "put time past" without seeing a soul, but when he awoke at night, the king's daughter was near him, and they talked awhile, and every morning when he got up, his suit of clothes was better and better, and so time was going past, till a year was nearly gone from the time he had left his mother.

304. Then his mother's spells and crosses began to work on him, and he could not but think on those he left behind.

305. On a night of these nights, while he lay chatting with the lady, he said that it was near a year and a day since he went away, and that his mother had laid crosses and spells upon him if he were alive and had the means that he should go back to see her and tell her his tale.

"I could easily find you a way to go," said she, "but my counsel is to stay."

But his mother's spells were always upon him, and so they talked and talked a great deal, and told their stories over again …

306. "I fear," said she at last, "that your mother will play you a trick that will harm us both, but tell me before you wish to start, and next day I will find you means to go."

307. The night came, and when he said that he must go, she said:

"When you rise you will find a new suit to put on, and food as usual, and you will find a black palfrey standing in the stable door, bridled and saddled, half in, half out, ready waiting for you. Mount, and she will take you where you wish to be. You have but to take off the bridle and let her go, and she will come home, but take good care not to lose the bridle. When you want to come back here, you have but to go out and shake the bridle, and the black palfrey will come for you."

308. As she said, so it was. He mounted, and he could not tell whether it was earth or air, till he arrived. But when he looked about he did not know the place; it was so altered with new houses.

309. He met an old man that he used to know, but he did not recognise him. He asked him where the old fisher lived.

"Oh," said the old man, "that man is not a fisherman now, he is richer than the king, and he has a house that is finer than the king's own."

Then he showed him the way, and as they went, the old man told the lad all that he could know of the story over again, and all that the lady had told the lad the night before, about the fisherman's changed life.

310. When he got to the grand new house, grooms came for the horse, but he said that he would stable the steed himself. He took off the bridle, and no one knew where the steed went.

311. Nobody knew him, but at last he showed the hair of his brow, and his mother knew him by a mote and a scar that were on his forehead, and then there was joy.

312. The king asked them all to dinner, and the king's eldest daughter fell in love with the fisher's son.

313. His mother wished him to marry the princess, but he would go back.

314. But before he went, his mother made him tell all his part of the story over again, and then she said:

"But have you seen what sort of creature she is?"

"No," said he, "I have not seen her. I have put my first sleep past before I perceive that she is near me, and I am in my sleep again when she goes away, and I never yet have seen what she is like."

315. "Well, my son," said the mother, "your pains seem great to me. You don't know whether she is black or white, nor what is her seeming. She may be legless for aught that you know, but here is a candle, it will light if you breathe your breath on it; keep it carefully till you get a chance, and when

she is asleep, light it. You will see whether it is worth your while to wait for her."

He took the candle, for he was glad to get it, and he put it next his breast.

316. Next morning he was up betimes, and went out, and shook his bridle, and came in to breakfast. But before he was well sat down, the black palfrey was beating on the door. He went out and bridled her, and mounted and started, and no one knew the way he went.

317. The black palfrey reached the golden castle, and he went in, and there he found the fire lit, and the board decked, and the candlestick with the lighted candle in it standing upon the board.

318. All things happened as was usual on the first night. On the second, when he awoke, he felt that something was near, so he spoke and the lady answered, and then they told the whole of their stories over again, so that no one might forget it, if repetition would serve that end.

319. "And now," said she, "beware of yourself, for the time is nearly run out."

"I will take good care," said he.

320. On the third night he took his candle from his breast, and hid it under the pillow, and when he awoke and spoke, none answered. Then he perceived that the lady slept, so he sought his candle and blew upon it with his breath, and it lit, and he saw the very sun-breath that was the most beautiful he ever had seen[86] laid asleep outside the clothes.

321. He was in great haste for fear she should wake, and he blew so hasty a blast at the candle that a spark fell upon her, and she went from him.

322. In an instant, each bed and castle and thing that was there was gone, and he, stripped as he was, lay on the ground with the seaman's clothes that he wore when he came beside him.

He had but to rise as fast as he could and put them on.

---

[86] *An aon deo-gréine bu bhòidhche:* a common phrase in speaking of a beautiful woman.

323. The castle was gone, and there was no knowing what had become of it.

The fisher's son was wandering far and wide about the wood, and he began to repent that he had not married the princess at home, for had he married her, he would not have lost thus both before and behind.

324. All that day he wandered in that wilderness of a wood, and when night came, he climbed a tree for fear wild beasts should be in the forest.

325. But when the night grew dark, the wild beasts were growling and whining all about the foot of the tree, and he feared that they would climb up and kill him. But no matter, that did not happen.

326. The second day he wandered about eating wild fruits, and when night came he climbed another tree, and the wild beasts growled and prowled about it.

327. When the third day came, the beasts left the root of the tree, and when daylight had come, he came down and set out to see what he might see in the forest. But he could see nothing save a wilderness of great trees.

328. At last he came to a pretty green grassy glade, and there he saw a lion, an eagle, and an ant at the carcase of an old white horse. At first he turned to flee from the lion, but the lion roared: "Stop, lad; you need not trouble to flee, for I could speedily catch you, but come hither and make fair division of this carcase between us three. If you judge fairly, you will profit and so shall we; but if you fail, we shall suffer hereafter."

So the lad went to the dead horse, and there he found a lion, an eagle, and an ant standing by the white carcase. He took his little rusty seaman's knife that he used to have when he fished with his father to split fish and make bait of limpets and buckies, and he thought awhile as he looked at the old horse. At last he took his knife and cut off the horse's head, and that he threw to the ant.

"Here, you ant," said he, "is your share; here you have food and shelter, store and store-house, and dwelling."

Then he took his knife again and ripped up the carcase and dragged out the inside, and that he threw to the eagle.

"There, you eagle," said he, "it is fittest and softest for you to rive and tear with beak and claws."

"And, you lion," said he, "take the rest, for you have most power and pith to strip flesh from bones with teeth and nails."

Then said the lion: "Well have you done; you have given each that which is fittest, and for that, if at any time you come to straits or peril and need, you may be a lion three times."

Then said the eagle: "You have helped me likewise, and if you have need and it will help you, you may be an eagle thrice."

Then said the ant: "He has aided me as much as either of you, and if ever he has need to be in small space or creep through crannies, he may be an ant thrice."

Then the three blessed him and he blessed the three, and he left them with the white carcase of the dead horse in the forest glade.

329. After this, one day, as he was wandering about the great forest, he thought that if he were an eagle, he would not be long ere he knew whether the house which held the daughter of the king of the golden castle was in the forest where he was. But no sooner did he think of the eagle than he was an eagle himself. He sprang, and he went upon his wings above the trees, and he wheeled and he wheeled about, and he wheeled round about again, and he saw the castle.

330. He flew away, and he perched upon the top of the castle till the night came. When the darkness was there, down he went and stood on the ground, and he went round about the castle and saw no one. He went to the door, but it was shut and barred.

331. He thought if he were as little as an ant that he would creep through the keyhole to see if the lady was there. But no sooner had he thought about the ant than he was one himself.

332. He climbed up the door and crept through the keyhole, and down the door to the floor, and in to the room where he used to find his food, but that room was dark, fireless, and without a candle. Then he crept on, climbing

doors and creeping through keyholes, till he crept through three chambers to the bedroom where he used to sleep, and there in the bed he heard a loud snore.

333. Then he understood that some one had got the place that he used to have.

334. The king's daughter knew that he was in the chamber, and she cried to a giant who was in the bed: "Get up, you giant; something that is not right is in the house."

335. The man who was in an ant climbed up the bed and fled into the hole of a wood-louse (*réudan*).

336. "I'll get him if he is inside this house," said the giant as he got up, "though he were no bigger than a barley-corn."

But the giant sought within and without, and all round about, and never thought that anyone could be in the hole of the wood-louse.

337. While he was gone, the other came out and took his own shape, and spoke to the lady and she to him. But they had small time to talk, for the giant came back, and the fisher's son had to go into the ant's shape and flee into the hole, and there he stayed till next night.

But the giant came grumbling back and said, "I found nothing within but what ought to be." And he went to sleep.

338. Next night the giant came in and slept, and the lady came in and laid herself where she was wont. Then the ant crept out and touched her with his sting.

"Rise, rise, giant," she cried aloud. "There is something about this castle that is not right, and unless you find it, it will harm either you or me."

But the ant fled back into the hole of the woodlouse.

"There is no one that can harm me," said the giant.

"Search the castle within and without," said she, "unless you find him, it will be the worse for you."

"There never was a man that could slay me," growled the giant, "but I'll go to seek him for you, and I will find him if he is no bigger than a barleycorn." And off he set to do the ransacking.

339. When he was gone the ant crept out and became a man, and he said:

"How do you do?" (*Cia mar a to thu*).

"Ill enough," said she. "Ill you have done to yourself and to me. Me you have lost, and my lot is to take this giant against my will. Oh, if you had been aware of yourself, it had been well with you and with me now, but I must bear my lot since it has fallen upon me."

"It was my mother's fault," said he.

"I know that," said she, "but if you had taken my counsel, you might have been married to me, with half the realm of the golden castle."

"Is there no way to get back?" said he.

"No, not while this giant lives," said she. And then they talked long and sadly, and told the story all over again.

340. "But," said the fisher's son, "perhaps I might find a way to slay this giant."

"You cannot slay him," said she. "It is not in himself that his life is at all."

"And where, then, is his life?" said the lad.

Said she: "It is in a lion that is in a thicket of oak, that is near the house of a farmer, that is at the uttermost end of this forest. In the lion's belly is a dove, and in the dove an egg. Nothing is that will kill this giant but to smite him with that egg."

341. Then they heard the clatter of the giant's feet coming, and the fisher's son had to be an ant a second time, and flee into the wood-louse's hole. The giant came in and sought in the room, and when he could find nothing, he went to bed and slept.

When the giant slept, the fisher's son crept out, for that was the last time he could be an ant, and it would not do to stay longer there. He thought the sooner he was out of the castle the better for him, so he climbed down the bed, and crept over the floor, and crawled up the door and through the keyhole, and down over the floors, and so from door to door, and from room to room, till he was outside the walls of the castle.

342. Then he thought of the eagle, and sprang and flew to the castle top, and there he sat till day.

343. As soon as the day came, he went upon his wrings to see if he could hit upon the farmer's house near the grove where the lion was.

344. *At the darkening of lateness* he got there and took his own shape, and he beat upon the door, and the farmer came out and said:

"Who are you, and whence?"

345. "I am a poor sailor," said he, "my ship was lost, and all on board were drowned but me; and since I cannot get back, I am seeking service."

"Come in, lad," said the farmer, "your sort used to be hungry and thirsty at times."

346. In he went, and from less to more he offered to be a herd. "We need one of your sort," said the farmer. A lion is in a thicket of wood near us, and each time the cattle go to that grove, the lion takes one of the cows, and sometimes he takes the best, and sometimes he takes the herd."

"I will be herd," said the fisher's son, and they settled the bargain.

347. Early in the morning he used to arise to put out the cattle. He drove them out and went with them to pasture where the grass was best, and at night he used to bring them home.

348. One of the farmer's daughters was dairymaid, and she fell in love with the herd, and she did not want him ever to go to the forest with the cattle, for fear that he should be slain by the lion.

349. On a day of these days, the herd said to the farmer: "I will go to the wood with the cattle today."

"Well, then, don't go too far in," said the farmer, "for fear that the lion should happen upon you and take one of the herd."

"I will take care of that," said the herdsman. The dairymaid did not wish him to go, but she was more afraid that the lion might take the lad. But no matter and never mind, the thing that was done was driving the cows to the wood.

350. When the herdsman got to the grove, instead of keeping the cows back, he drove them farther and farther into the forest, till at last the lion came.

351. He was going to seize a brindled heifer that was there, but the herd got between them.

352. Then he thought on the lion that he helped at the white horse, and in the twinkling of an eye, he was a lion himself.

353. The two lions struggled till the sun was going west beneath the mountain at evening, without knowing which was losing or winning.

354. They could struggle no more, so they sat and stared at each other.

355. "If I had a draught of water I would rive you to gobbets," said the forest lion.

356. "If I had one of wine I would tear you to tatters asunder," said the herd lion.

Then the forest lion got up and stalked back to the wood again, and then the herd lion got up and made a herd of himself, and drove the cattle home, singing a ditty tunefully.

357. When he got home, the farmer said: "How went it with you to-day?"

"Well," said he.

"Saw you the lion?" said the master.

"I saw him," said the herd.

"I wonder he did not take one of the cattle," said the farmer.

"He wanted to take one," said the herd, "but I would not let him."

358. The cattle were sent to the byre, and the dairymaid milked them.

359. And she never got so much milk from them before.

360. The herd got well taken to that night. Joy and a feast were made for him.

361. Next day the master said: "You need not go to the wood with the beasts. A day now and again is enough. It is not easy tó keep cows from the lion." The dairymaid said as much for fear of the herd's life.

But he said:

"There is good grass in the groves, and it is best to hold on till the cattle make it bare. I will keep off the lion."

362. "Then I will go with you," said the farmer's daughter, and she was ready to start, but he would not let her go that day.

363. He drove the cattle farther and farther in, till the lion came as before, and tried at the brindled heifer.

364. Then the herd ran between and thought on the lion, and was a lion himself. The two lions struggled and tugged and fought all day, till the sun was going down under the mountain at evening, and then at last they paused and gazed.

365. "If I had a draught of water," said the forest lion, "I would tear you to tatters."

366. "If I had a draught of wine," quoth the lion-herd, "I would not be long about riving you asunder."

367. Then they got up and went their ways as before.

368. "Saw you the lion?" said the farmer, as he got home.

"I saw him," said the herd, "and he wanted to take the brindled heifer, but I hindered him."

"It's odd that he did not take you," said the master.

"If he could, he would have done that same," quoth the herd.

369. So much milk they never got before.

370. And the herd was feasted, and praised, and well treated that night.

371. Next morning the farmer said: "I rather incline to think that you had better set the cattle on some other way to-day. A day in the wood now and again is quite enough. It is rather risky to go often to the forest with them, but that's no matter."

"The best grass is in the woods," said the herd, "and it is best to go there that grass may grow elsewhere."

372. The dairymaid did all she could to keep the herd from the wood, for fear that he should be killed by the lion, but no matter. To the wood they went.

373. Instead of holding the cattle back, he drove them farther and farther in, till the lion came, and he, as was his wont, tried to take the best in the herd. The herdsman thought of the lion for whom he divided the carcase, and was a lion for the third time, and the two lions struggled. And they struggled, and fought, and hauled, and pulled, and dragged, and bit, and roared, and growled, and struggled again, till the sun was almost near going under the hill, and neither knew which should win or lose.

374. Then they ceased struggling, and sat and glowered.

375. "If I had one draught of water, you should never more keep me from taking a cow: I would tear you to pieces," said the forest lion.

376. "If I had a draught of wine, I would set you so that you should never more come to take a cow that belonged to another, for I would rive you to gobbets."

377. Who should be at his back when he spoke but the farmer's daughter coming to him with wine to freshen him up, for it seemed to her that he was weary on the night before. And she gave him the draught of wine.

378. The forest lion rose and fled. The other rose when he had drunk his wine, and he stretched out after him, and he caught him, and killed him, and tore him to pieces.[87]

379. The pigeon came out of the lion's belly and sprang away on her wings. But the lion-herd made an eagle of himself for the third time, and spread his wings and darted after her, and he caught her and killed her, and took the bits to pieces, and found the egg.

380. He never went back to the farmer's daughter or to the cows, but on he flew to the castle, where was the daughter of the king of the golden castle, and when he got there, he got into his own shape.

381. He went into the castle, and into the room where he used to find food, but there was none there, and on he went through the other chambers till he reached the bedroom.

382. There lay the giant with *ich* and *och* and *acain*, groaning in a miserable plight.

383. When the fisher's son went into the chamber where the giant was, he got up to be at grips with him. But he cast the egg at him, and the egg struck the giant full in the front of his face, and down tumbled the giant, dead.

384. The hardest work the fisher's son ever found to do, was to carry that giant out of the castle. He tried to lift him, but he could not stir him. The thing which he had to do at last, was to take his seaman's knife and cut him into four quarters, and carry him out bit by bit, and bury him in a hole that he happened to find somewhere outside.

385. When that was done and the chamber cleaned, he went and sat where he was wont, and there he sat till night.

---

[87] The equivalent of the mermaid's death. This lion was one of the tribe who guarded the hearts of mythical beings

386. When the night darkened, the candlestick with the lighted candle in it came and stood on the board as it used to do. When he wished for food he had it instantly, and when he grew sleepy and wished to rest, the candlestick and the candle showed him the way, and he went to bed and slept.

387. When he awoke he felt that some creature was near him. He spoke, and the king's daughter answered.

"Are you to be mine if I make out the time?" said he.

"I am," said she, "but you must begin at the beginning and be as you are for a year and a day. If you do that I shall be yours, and the golden realm—all as you might have had it before, unless you think it too long to wait."

"I am willing to wait if I get you then," said he.

"You will," said she, "if you wait, and you shall have all you wish for here but me while you are waiting for me."

388. "I'll do that," said he, and so he did. Nothing worth telling happened for a year and a day, which seemed like one day to a lonely man who saw no one. At the end of the time, as he was wandering about in the castle, wearying, in came the most beautiful darling of a woman that he ever had seen, and said—

389. "I am the daughter of the king of the golden castle, and now I am free of the spells that held me, but I must be gone for three days."

390. "I will take you to the realm where my father is. This is not my castle, this is an enchanted castle, and we must leave it soon. Stay here till I come back."

391. He did not like that at all, but for fear that he might go wrong as he did before, he stayed there all alone for three days, and he never said a word against it.

392. Then she came forth with a band of maidens and of youths, and she said: "I have come to seek you to go to the golden realm with me."

393. "The ship is ready, let us go." And so they sailed over the ocean to the golden realm, where the old king was pleased to see his daughter come back with a handsome lad, and there they were married.

THE MEETING OF THE THREE WAYS.

394. So the fisher's three sons, who went upon three ways by courage, cunning, and patience, by using gifts earned from thrice three talking creatures of earth and air, had conquered nine foes. They had overcome three giants with many heads, and a giantess, owners of three metallic castles; a dragon with three heads who came from the sea; a mermaid whose life was in an egg which was won from the sea; the great Turk, his army, and his fleet, which brought him from the sea; a lion, in three hard fights, who wished for water and therefore belonged to the sea; a giant who could only be slain with an egg which came out of the lion. Each had won a princess and was heir to a kingdom; one had got three metallic castles besides, and they had overcome six fortresses. Now they have to encounter the weakest, and the least, and the most dangerous of their foes in the seventh castle. And this is the way in which the story was told in the Isles.

THE MEETING OF THE FISHER'S THREE SONS.

395. On a day of these days the fisher's eldest son got early up and looked out of the window, and saw a little black castle over against him, and he asked his wife what castle that might be.

396. She said it was but a castle that an evil creature had, and that no one ever came back who went there.

397. "No matter," said he, "I will go."

"There never went a man there that came back to tell a tale," said she.

"I will see who dwells there," said the fisher's eldest son.

So up he got and took his black horse and dog, and over he went to the castle without more ado.

398. He went in, and there he saw a woman combing her hair.

"Whence comest thou, father of my fondness and mother of my love, come up till thou tell me thy tale, come till I tell thee mine," quoth she. With many flattering words she wiled him on till he went towards her.

399. Then she snatched up her magic club and smote him and made him a pillar of stone.

400. She did the same to the horse and the hound, and there they all lay.

401. Now the old fisherman looked every day at his three trees in the garden, and one day he looked and saw that one had lost its leaves.

"That's true," said he, "I have lost a son this day."

402. "I," said the middle son, who had come home, "I am going away to raise my brother's *éric* or blood-fine."

403. He mounted his black horse, and his black dog followed him. His father had put a fish-bone in his hand, and it had grown into the gold-hilted glaive that hung at his side, and that had given him learning and wisdom. Away he went; each road was crooked, and every path smooth, and the black dog ran the track straight and right to the herd's hut.

404. There never were created two more alike than he and his brother.

405. "What made you stay away from your wife and sweetheart last night?" said the old herd.

406. He was sent up to the king's house. The king's daughter went to meet him and to embrace him, believing him to be her own husband.

407. He did not know how in the world he could manage to keep from his brother's chamber that night.

408. So he told his brother's wife that he had laid a heavy wager with a gentleman, so that he could not go to bed, but he would sleep on a table in front of the bed. And he did so till morning.

409. Then when he looked out, he saw the little black castle, and said to her: "What is yonder castle?"

Said she: "Did I not tell you that last night?" And then she told him all about it, and tried to keep him from going there.

410. But he rose and went out, took his horse and hound, and over he went to the castle.

411. In he went, and as was done to his brother, so was it done to him.

412. The old fisher looked out in the morning, and the leaves had fallen from the middle tree.

413. "That's true," said the youngest brother, who had come home in haste, "my brother is not alive. I will begone to raise his *éric*."[88]

414. He took his horse and hound and gold-hilted sword which his father gave him with learning and wisdom, and off he set. Each road was even and each path smooth for him, and he rode, and ran right and straight up to the palace of the king of the Greeks.

415. The princess saw him out of the window, and out she went to meet and welcome and embrace him, and took him home.

416. "It was enough to stay away the first night, without staying from me yesternight again," said she.

"Many a man may have matters of moment with gentlefolks, so that it may not be known when he will come," said the lad.

417. They went to rest, and he laid a cold sword between them.

418. In the morning he cast his eyes away from him, and saw the castle as his brothers had seen it, and asked what castle that might be.

419. "Did I not tell you that last night and the night before?" said she, and then she told him.

420. He arose, and took his horse and hound, and over he went to the castle. In he went, and he too saw a woman combing her hair.

---

[88] It occurs in the "Ramayana," on the occasion of a great horse-sacrifice. In Swedish stories too: *svennen lade ett blankt svärd på bädden mellum sig och henne.*

421. "Come up, treasure,"[89] said she, "son of the father of my desire, and the mother of my love, till I tell thee my news, and thou tellest me thine."

422. He had no good notion of her, so he sprang towards her and felled her, and put his cold sword-edge upon her throat. "Death's overhead," said he, "what's your *éric?*"

423. "That's much," said she. "A chest of gold and a chest of silver."

"That's mine," said he, "and thy death." And he whipped off her head.

424. But as he did, his sword flew out of his hand.

425. Then the old woman grasped her head in both her hands and set it upon her throat where it was before.

426. The dog sprang at her, but she smote him with the magic club, and down he fell.

427. Then the lad gripped the crone, and they wrestled and struggled, till he wrested the magic club from her hand.

428. Then he smote her, and down she fell dead.

429. He took her keys from her and searched the house.

430. He found one chamber full of gold and one full of silver.

431. He found a chamber full of gentlefolks' dresses.

432. And one full of saddles, (433) and bridles, (434) and one full of boots and shoes.

435. He found a room full of men turned into pillars of stone,

---

[89] *Fheudail.*

436. and a vessel of balsam for bringing to life again.

437. Then he took and began to spill it upon them till he revived them all; and amongst them were his own brothers.

438. He gave his clothes and his own share to every man that was there, and a lot of gold and silver, and when all that was done the three brothers went off to the palace.

439. Then the youngest said to the eldest, "You have the best wife that the dew of heaven ever was shed upon."

440. "How know you that?" said he.

"I was with her last night," said the youngest brother.

441. Then black jealousy struck the eldest, and he turns to him and sweeps off his head with his sword.

442. The old fisherman looked out at his garden, and the tree of the youngest had fallen and the other two stood.

"That's true," said he. "The youngest is dead, and the other two live again."

443. The brothers stayed that night in the palace, and in the morning they went away in a coach.

444. They went home to their father's house, and took him and their mother, and in the morning they put them in a castle by themselves.

445. The eldest brother got the realm, and the king's daughter was his wedded wife, and there these two lived happily, according to Alasdair mac Ruairidh Bhain.

446. What became of the other and of the castles which were won, and the kingdoms, this narrator cannot tell, but some day or other he hopes to hear more about them out in the Isles.

NOTES TO CELTIC DRAGON MYTH

Number of Notes apply to the Numbered Sections.

1. If Duncan's house was not like that, Donald MacPhie's house, in which I heard this story told in South Uist, was, and Donald told me that Duncan the fisher lived in Skye.

Others say that he lived in the "Green Isle," which is a kind of Gaelic Paradise out in the West. A version of the "Green Isle" from the Tiree tradition is given in the *Scottish Historical Review* for 1908.

Sometimes a fisherman or a sailor, or a smith who is also a fisherman, almost always a poor man who lives near the sea, in Gaelic; in Italian (*Straparola*), a poor couple; in Swedish, a smith and a fisherman; in Russian, a poor man.

4. *Mouth of night.*—This phrase has a relation in Sanskrit, and is the common Gaelic equivalent for a nightfall.

Mermaid.—Near the Clyde where ships abound and old sailors tell this tale in bits, the mermaid becomes a ship which anchors near the boat, and the iron is bought for gold dust which the sailors shoved out of the ports till the boat is ready to sink. Sometimes the bargain is struck for the first thing that touches the fisher's knee when he lands, and that is his infant son.

According to authorities quoted by Fergusson (*Tree and Serpent Worship*, p. 35), it is a custom in Dahomey to sacrifice a man occasionally to Hu, the god of the sea. The man is carried in a hammock from the capital dressed as a noble, a canoe takes him to sea, and he is thrown to the sharks.

143

In one Swedish version, the smith meets a troll maiden in the forest, and by her has a son, who is the supernatural hero. In others the hero is otherwise mysteriously born.

In Russian, the hero is simply a poor man's youngest, lazy, despised son. In the East a gift son, who is an incarnation of some divinity, occurs frequently. In the "Ramayana" (p. 20, vol. ii., *History of India*, by Talboys Wheeler), sons are born after eating divine food, the gift of the gods. The childless Maharaja causes a horse sacrifice to be performed. After the rite an Emanation of Brahma appears with a golden vessel filled with rice and milk—pyassa, the essence of the sacrifice, the food of the gods. Three wives eat of the food, and give birth to four sons, who are incarnations of Vishnu. These divine men were born to overcome Ravana, the king of demons. He oppressed gods and men, and was invulnerable to celestials. He had ten heads and twenty arms, copper-coloured eyes, and a polished body. He lived in Ceylon, amongst gold and jewels. Amongst his numerous feats he went to Bagavati, the great city of resplendent serpents, and carried off the wife of the snake Takshaka. He afterwards carried off Sita, the wife of Rama, and was overcome. A far older form of this notion of a gift-son will be found in the Aitareya Brahmana of the "Rig Veda" (*Haug*, 1863, p. 460). King Harischandra wished for a son, and addressed a verse to Narada, who replied in ten verses. The king then went to King Varuna (the god of waters, and therefore the equivalent of the western mermaid) and prayed for a son, promising to sacrifice him to Varuna. Varuna claimed the son when he was born; at ten days old; when his teeth had come; when they had fallen out; when they had come again; when he had got his arms:—six times. When the son was told that he was to be sacrificed, he ran away to the wilds. After six years of wandering, and after meeting Indra, the chief of gods in human form, several times, Rohita, the victim, bought a human substitute, Sunahsepa, the son of a poor Brahman, for a hundred cows. The boy was accepted by Varuna and was prepared for sacrifice. His father was to slay him. On repeating hymns he was released by the gods, became a priest, and was promoted to be heir. The resemblance of this very ancient Hindu legend to the history of Abraham is very remarkable. According to accepted chronology, a period of from 500 to 700 years lies between the compilation of the Brahmanas and the birth of Isaac. The distance between the Punjab and the land of Abraham is about half as great as the distance traversed in a few years by Alexander the Great on his march to India. So the Hebrew history may have originated the whole series which extends from East to West.

In the "Vedas" many verses allude to the birth of gift sons to childless sages by the special favour of the celestial powers invoked in these ancient hymns.

These references will serve to show how widely spread the legend is in the East and West, and how closely connected the whole series of tradition is with holy writ. In the Russian story the hero fights a dragon, his two sons, and his wife; of these one transforms himself into a well, and another into an apple tree, a third into a cushion. By running the scent eastwards we thus get very near serpent worship and tree worship; and an Indian custom founded upon the subjugation of the serpent races by Aryans. In some States the fair-skinned Aryan Raja at his accession mingles his own blood with blood from the arm of a dark-skinned man of the subject races of aboriginal serpent worshippers. Of these races many still adore serpents; of old the worship pervaded all India (see Fergusson on *Tree and Serpent Worship*, and other books of authority on this curious subject). In 1876, while wandering in India, I found the serpent worshipped all over the country, at Benares and everywhere.

5. This incident in various shapes occurs in the Swedish collection as was told in various parts of Sweden and in Finland. The fish generally is a pike. But in these regions pike generally live in the sea, which in the Gulf of Bothnia is brackish. In Hindu legend Vishnu took the form of a fish and related the history of creation and the deluge.

6. In the Swedish and German collections and in others the wife is a grumbler.

9. *The Fisher.*—Told by Alexander MacNeill, fisherman, Ceann Tangaval, Barra; Alasdair Mac Ruaraidh Bhain to Hector Maclean, 1859.

The Fisher's Son.—Twice told by John MacPhie in South Uist to J. F. Campbell, 1859, 1860.

The cow also got a bit, according to MacPhie.

"West Highland Tales," No. IV., told by John Mackenzie, fisherman, near Inveraray, to Hector Urquhart and to J. F. Campbell.

Compare Grimm ("Gold Children," p. 241) and various versions in Swedish. In most versions there are but two mysteriously born heroes. In one Swedish version three are born of three maidens who drank from a well.

The sons result from the eating of two enchanted apples in one Swedish story, and from drinking at a well in another. They are sons of a princess and her maiden who are shut up in a tower.

11. The sons are twins in one Gaelic version which I have. From the sequel these ought to be twins; in home and foreign versions they are twins.

In "The Fisher," the Gaelic version which I followed as most complete, the birth of each son is told in the same way, nearly in the same words, so they are not twins, but a leash of sons growing up a year apart, each to succeed the other. Taking all I know about this story, I think that the sons ought to be born together, so I have shortened my story by two repetitions.

(2) *Straparola.*—They adopt a foundling. In the "Ramayana" four sons are born to a childless old Raja by three wives, who eat pyassa, the rice and milk of the gods, which is brought from heaven in a golden vessel by a celestial being who steps out of the fire. These sons are incarnations of Vishnu. Only three play conspicuous parts in the Hindu epic, so I suspect that three was the original number of brothers and that the story is Aryan, older than the Hindu epics, and older than the Celtic migration from the East.

12. This incident occurs in one Gaelic version only. Possibly this may be the enemy who fights the smith's son afterwards in the shape of the dragon. He may be the servant or second sailor or second character in other versions; he may be the same character as the Swedish hero who was son of Smith and troll maiden of the forest. In the Russian version of the dragon-slaying story

the dragon left a wife and two sons to be slain afterwards, of whom one was a well and the other a tree.

Probably this sea-baby is one of them, and a water-serpent myth.

13. "West Highland Tales," No. IV., as told by John Mackenzie. This is like Varuna, see note on 4.

15. Horses and hounds fourteen years of age vitiate the unities. But in some versions of this story the heroes set out as soon as they are born. See "Shortshanks" in *Norse Tales*. Being gift-children, they probably were superhuman at first.

18. In Swedish the smith forges three swords of enormous weight, the last the biggest and heaviest. In Russian, Ivan of the Ashes makes for himself three iron clubs of like proportions and weights. The incident is common in many Gaelic stories and varies exceedingly. In other Swedish versions the swords are otherwise acquired. All agree in making these iron weapons.

19. This from the telling of a lad near Inveraray.

20. From the same Inveraray lad. Compare "A Sop for Cerberus." A similar incident is in a story of Fionn, who went to Scandinavia and there captured a mighty hound. The hounds of the Fenians are very mythical and play a large part in the Fenian Romance. Some of them are transformed human creatures. In that they resemble Hindu avatars such as Hunymàn the divine monkey.

26. From *An Gille Glas* (p. 370). In Swedish the lad is angry because his father did not make the first sword heavy enough. In Russian the lad tosses the iron clubs so high that they are up for days, and catches them on his forehead. Two break, the third nearly knocks him down; so he is satisfied. Indian jugglers in fact cast cocoa-nuts high into the air and catch them on their foreheads, where they break. It is a common athletic performance.

29. In the "Rig Veda Saṅhita" (Wilson's trans.) it appears that Indra's weapon, the thunderbolt, was originally made of the bones of a man. This

may indicate the use of bone weapons and of ivory clubs by ancient tribes in the East and West or at the centre of the Aryan migrations.

The incident of trees which live while brothers live, and wither and warn their mother when they die, is in a central American myth given in "Popul Vuh."

In Russian the hero leaves gloves which drop blood when he is in straits. In Swedish and in other languages he gives a knife which drips blood or rusts. The token with this property varies, but the life of man and tree accords best with Indian ideas about tree worship. A man told me in India that he had been present at the marriage of a pet plant to a divinity with all ceremony.

31. *Straparola.*—The foundling discovers his origin and goes to seek his fortune with a horse and a sword.

32. Told by Margaret MacFhingon, in the island of Berneray, Sound of Harris, to Hector Maclean. She learned the story from John Morrison in Rusgary, Berneray, who, in August 1859, was a tenant in North Uist. Her story follows one son—not the oldest—on the way to fortune by courting and courage.

34. In Swedish the hero is followed by beasts but they are otherwise obtained. So it is in German. This transformation occurs in Gaelic and in Italian.

Lion, Falcon, Wolf.—John MacPhie, S. Uist, "W. H. Tales," vol. i., 94.

Wolf, Hoodie, Fox, Smith's Son.—The creatures vary to suit the incidents in the sequel, and these are associated with the herding of cattle with castles won from giants by brute force, and with the slaying of the dragon. In other stories they are Great Dog, Falcon, Otter (p. 73, vol. i.), Hector Urquhart; John Mackenzie, Inveraray.

Lean Hound of the Green Wound, Falcon, Otter.—The Young King of Easaidh Ruaidh.—Maclean; James Wilson; MacQueen, Islay, about 1810.

From "The Smith's Son," told by B. MacAskill, an old wife in Berneray, to Hector Maclean.

In "Straparola" the foundling with horse and sword meets (*a*) lion, (*b*) eagle, (*c*) ant, (*d*) fox, when he divides a carcase, (*e*) who grant him the power to take their shapes.

35. (1) A castle, (2) a castle, (3) a gentleman, (4) the capital of France, (5) a king's house, (6) a king's house, (7) a king's house, (8) the king of the Greeks.

In "Straparola," he goes to a palace where he is a poor man. Here the Italian story branches to the second brother's adventures.

In Swedish the lad goes to be cook's mate at the king's house and hides his three swords under a stone. In other versions he takes other service. Sometimes he is herd.

36. This varies exceedingly, but the place chosen seems to fit the sequel, and the sequel here is herding.

Since this story was translated I have found that the state myth of Japan is like the Gaelic dragon myth. A man came to a house where all were weeping, and learned that the last daughter of the house was to be given to a dragon with seven or eight heads who came to the sea-shore yearly to claim a victim. He went with her, enticed the dragon to drink "sake" (*vice* wine) from pots set out on the shore, and then he slew the monster. From the end of his tail he took out a sword, which is supposed to be the Mikado's state sword. He married the maiden, and with her got a jewel or talisman which is preserved with the regalia. A third thing of price so preserved is a mirror. See "My Circular Notes"(Macmillan, 1876).

37. (1) A swine herd, (2) a herd, (3) a herd, (4) a farmer, (5) a herd, (6) a cook, (7) a king's herd, (8) a herd.

In Swedish also the service varies much; this Gaelic version about winning the castles is not in the Swedish collection. One brother wins a castle, but not in this way. He wins it by befriending ants, bees, and ducks.

In Norse, Shortshanks serves in the kitchen. In the "Mahabharata," a famous Indian epic, five brothers disguise themselves and take service (1) as dice-player, (2) as cook, (3) as herd, (4) as groom, (5) as music and dancing master in the women's apartments. Their joint wife serves the queen. They leave their arms on a tree and at need sally forth and perform great feats of valour.

In another part of the same story Bhima, the strong brother, then disguised as a mendicant, saves a Brahman's child from a monster who exacted tribute of food and a human being daily. Bhima acts cook and glutton, and this brother is like him in many ways.

In 1876 I was shown from Kungva a great white snow patch high up on the Dhaoladhan range, which was said to be the tomb of the dragon slain by Bhima. The hero promised him honourable burial if he fought well and kept his word, and gave him a white coffin when he had vanquished the dragon. That tract of country is pervaded by myths of the "Mahabharata."

38. *A park, a glen, a forest.*—The best version here is the "Gray Lad" as told by John Smith in South Uist—so that is followed.

39 -44. In Gaelic this new character is elsewhere called "The Five-Headed Giant," a big giant, a "Fuath" or fiend, a big man, a forest lion. He is variously described, but in character is the punisher of trespassers and the cattle-lifters' enemy. It is not easy to select the original of this character amongst the crowds of enemies slain by mythical heroes, but here are some of the most conspicuous. (1) In the "Vedas," the oldest of Eastern Sanskrit compositions, Ahi, Vritra, and the Panis stole the cows of the gods. Indra slew the monster Ahi, and rescued the cows. (2) In the oldest of Sanskrit epics, the "Mahabharata," Raja Suserman carried off the cows of Raja Vivata from Sahadeva, a hero disguised as a herd. Bhima, another hero disguised as a cook, defeated the enemy and rescued the cows. (3) In the "Ramayana," another famous Sanskrit epic, Ravana, king of demons,

married to the wife of a great serpent, dwelt in Ceylon in Lanka, a city with seven walls made of iron, stone, brass, white-metal, copper, silver, gold; and full of jewels, dresses, magical treasures, and weapons. Ravana had ten heads, twenty arms, copper-coloured eyes, and a body like polished onyx. He carried off Sita, the wife of Rama, and Rama, aided by birds, bears, and monkeys, who were avatars or incarnations of the gods, slew him. On the whole, this looks very like an elaborate Eastern version of the tale which is preserved in the West in this form. (4) In Norse the trolls who confronted Shortshanks had many heads. (5) In Swedish it was the same. (6) In Russian the same. (7) In classical mythology Jupiter overcame Typho, a giant with a hundred serpents' heads. (7) Hercules slew the Lernean hydra. (8) There are many similar characters in ancient and modern mythology, but on the whole Ravana in the "Ramayana" is most like these Highland giants. The tale probably came West, and this many-headed giant probably grew where the idea of Sesha Naga began to grow amongst blacks. According to Hindu mythology, he is a king of snakes, and rules in a real underground; he supports the world upon his thousand heads; he owns riches, and the water of life, and a jewel that restores the dead to life. He probably represents the serpent worship of the Aborigines whom the Aryans overcame in India. (9) Gormundgandr, the great sea snake of the "Edda" who encircles the world, is another Western form of the same myth. (10) Many-headed Naga Rajus and men with hoods made by the hooded heads of the mythical snakes which wait upon them are figured abundantly in Fergusson's book upon Tree and Serpent Worship. They are sculptured at many places in Ceylon (v. my "Circular Notes"). (11) A version of this part of the Highland story is current on the east coast of Africa.

In "Sultan Darai" (*Swahili Tales told at Zanzibar*, Bell and Duldy, 1870) a ruined man buys a gazelle with a coin which he finds in a dust-heap. The gazelle plays Puss in Boots. He finds a jewel, takes it to a sultan as a gift from his master, asks the sultan's daughter for him, fetches him to the place, bathes him, beats him, strips him, and leaves him. He goes to the sultan, gets clothes for his master, and marries him to the princess. Then he goes to find a fit dwelling for Sultan Darai. He found a deserted town, a palace, and an old woman who is the equivalent of the servant in this story. From her he learned that this is the town and house of a great snake with seven heads, who is rich in jewels like Ravana and the Highland giants. When he comes every second day, at noon, he comes in a storm of wind and dust, as the dragon of the West comes in wind and spray. He eats and comes to a well in his house to drink at noon. He has a sword like a flash of lightning, that hangs on a peg. The gazelle took it. The snake smelt him. The old woman said that she has scented herself. The snake puts his seven heads one after the other; the gazelle smote them off in a fearful turmoil, and fainted. He found rooms full of food and full of provisions and slaves and goods, and he said to the old woman, "Do you keep these goods till I ask my master, he is the owner of these goods."

Zanzibar is frequented by Indian sailors, and by Arabs, and by traders from Central Africa. It is manifest that this is the same story, and that it is impossible now to say whence the dragon myth of the West came, or who was the type of the giant with many heads. Probability is in favour of a non-Aryan origin and serpent worship by aboriginals.

(12) The state myth of Japan includes the many-headed monster, the sword, and jewel of this African tale.

N.B.—Brahma, Vishnu, and Shiv are represented with serpent hoods on old temples near the sources of the Ganges.

46. In the "Mahabharata," Sahadeva, one of the Pandavas, became herd to Raja Vivata, and the cows yielded three or four times as much milk as they had ever done before (210, *History of India*).

39-67. This part is taken chiefly from "The Gray Lad," as told by John Smith, labourer, in South Uist, to Hector Maclean, and written by him. (2) Some incidents and variations are taken from the version which was twice told to J. F. C. with a year's interval by Donald MacPhie, a very old man in South Uist. (3) Some incidents are taken from the version told by John Mackenzie, fisherman, near Inveraray, written by Hector Urquhart, gamekeeper at Ardkinglas. (4) Some fragments are from the versions told to J. F. C. Some of the incidents in this part are, in the Swedish collection, attributed not to land-people, but to sea-dragons. Of these, one asks "if this mannikin will kill him as he killed his brothers." It is in the last degree improbable that this can have been taken directly from the "Ramayana" or from any book. It is therefore exceedingly remarkable to find so much in common in East and West.

68-75. As yet I have been unable to find the Eastern equivalent of this fourth character, the hideous wife of one many-headed monster, and the mother of two. Ravana had a mother, but she did not come out to fight. It is curious if the Western story preserves more characters than the Eastern epics.

[Since this was written I have been to India, and now think that Kali, the wife of Shiva, may be the original or another form of the original of the terrible hag of the Gaelic tales.]

75. *Glas* in this translation, but anything that shines may be the meaning, say polished armour.

77-175. According to different versions, the next enemy to be overcome is in Gaelic (1) The five-headed giant, (2) a beast [Smith's son], (3) a beast [The Gray Lad], (4) the eldest son of the King of Sorcha [The Fisher], (5) a dragon [The Mermaid], (6) a dragon [MacPhie], (7) three giants [Irish fiddler].

In all cases he is a sea-creature, and in all he is superhuman. In one Swedish version three princesses have to be rescued from three sea-dragons with three, six, twelve heads, who came for them because the king had promised his daughter to a sea-troll in a storm. This indicates human sacrifices to sea-gods. In other Swedish versions the dragon has fifty heads. In one only he lives on a rock inland, and there he spits fire. In Norse three trolls with five, ten, fifteen heads came in ships for the princess. These are the equivalents of the "Sons of the King of Sorcha" in Gaelic. In Sanskrit this part is played in the "Mahabharata" by the Asura Raja Vaka, to whom the people of Ekuchakra were forced daily to send a man and a great quantity of provisions to be devoured under a banyan tree. A Brahman had to supply the victim Bhima, the strong brother of the (5) Pandavas, who lived with the Brahman as mendicants, fought the monster with clubs and trees and fists, and tore him asunder by main force. Then he secretly disappeared, with his mother and his four brothers (v. p. 112 of Wheeler's *History of India*). Wheeler says that this fiction is a striking reflex of the Hindu mind. It is

Western as well as Eastern. This, of course, is the story of St George and the Dragon which has got into Christian legends all over Europe; see "Dragons and Dragon-slayers" in Good Words for April and May 1870. Indra slays Ahi; Vritra, Asuras, blackmen, serpents, Dasyus, Panis, and other mythical foes in "Vedas." Bhima overcomes Vaka, and the Kauravas and many other foes in the "Mahabharata." Rama overcomes Ravana; Nala overcomes Kali the great serpent; Jupiter beats Typho; Ulysses kills Polyphemus; Arthur and Fionn slay boars and robbers and mythical foes. According to theorists, all three mean that light fights dark, summer winter, good evil, life death; or fair people dark serpent-worshippers. It is impossible as yet to decide what is the origin of the dragon myth, but the Gaelic version of it is here given and it is very full of incident. Of course this is the same myth as that of Perseus and Andromeda, which also is a water myth with a flying horse in it. The oldest known form of the slaying of a monster by a hero appears to be a water myth, for after the slaying of Ahi by Indra the rains came down and the rivers flowed. There was a dog-fight in that ancient myth, and a herd's dog which tracked the stolen cows.

In the Russian equivalent of this story, the hero slays serpents with three, six, and twelve heads. There is darkness in the land because of the serpents; after the battle there is light. Three brothers, of whom the youngest is the hero, then go out and conquer the snakes, children, and widow They transform themselves into cushions in a meadow, apples on trees, and a fountain. The elder brother went to rest on the cushions to eat the apples and to drink of the well. The youngest smites them with his iron club, and they turn to blood. This explains one bit of the Gaelic legend in which three personages overcome by the hero are three sons of the King of Sorcha or Light, who is manifestly a mythological personage. The dragon represented in Japanese pictures of this story which I have seen in Japan comes in a cloud of driving rain, and has fiery eyes. Manifestly he is meant for a storm fiend. I suppose that the myth may be traced to a personification of a sacred river with many "mouths" and many "heads." The Chinese dragon pictured on walls in Canton, and embroidered on dresses, is a water dragon like all the rest.

78. Sometimes he drives the cows to the strand and is still the herd; sometimes he breakfasts with the old herd. He always eats, like Bhima the strong hungry brother in the "Mahabharata."

79. The character of Boaster is played in the "Mahabharata" by Raja Vivata, who claims victories won by Bhima as cook, and by Arjuna as music and dancing master. The part is played by various characters in the West. In Swedish it is a tailor; in Norse a red ritter. In other versions of the story it is a great general; this is from the "Five-Headed Giant" from Berneray.

80. In Swedish there was a great turmoil of waves. In Norse the wind whistles after the ship. This Gaelic description is fuller than any other, probably because of familiarity with Atlantic weather and marine landscape. In Japan a storm is depicted, and is described: when the dragon was slain the storm ended.

82. The mark varies in foreign stories—sometimes a ring is fastened to the hair. In Gaelic the mark is the "lugmark" of the shepherd and herdsman almost invariably where this incident occurs, and it is common to many stories.

90. In Swedish each of three sea dragons with a superfluity of heads was attended by a dog "as big as a calf," "as big as an ox," "as big as any beast." Previous to the great battle there is a dog-fight, and the lad's dog is swallowed in the last. In another Gaelic story this incident also appears, and the swallowed dog likewise appears through the hound who is slain. There is no sea-dog in any Gaelic version yet found—May 1870.

97. In Swedish and in Norse the hero goes back to his service and says nothing. He gives gold rings and pearls and other spoil to the cook or kitchenmaid, his chief; and the boaster gets the credit. In Swedish the king thinks of a similar proverb: "Oft sits the scarlet heart under the Vadmal cloak," i.e., a noble heart under hodden gray. In the "Mahabharata" the Pandavas slink off and return to their disguises and disappear.

131. From a version told by Dewar and MacNair. In Swedish the princess aids by putting rags on the necks of the monster, for the heads when they

touch water gain life and hop on again. This incident is in Gaelic also, and occurs at the end of this story.

139. Sometimes he is forgotten. In Swedish he is found in the kitchen by three princesses, is sent for, and won't go. In Norse the princess desires him to pour out wine; he does at the feast, and is there revealed in glorious dresses given him by the princess. In Gaelic he wins his own braveries and three castles to boot. A dress of honour is part of the story always.

140. From the Fisher.

141. In other tales this part is played by a great eagle. The whistle and the yellow-faced servant, a flying horse, and all the rest of this indicates a genius and an Eastern origin. In Swedish and in German the hero sends his creatures—fox, wolf, bear, and so on—to fetch food, drink, and other tokens from the palace.

142. This ought to be the wishing cloth, but it is not in any version of the story yet got except as above. I have not found it in any foreign version either.

143. From the Fisher and the Gray Lad.

162. …A magnificent vehicle with as many horses harnessed to it as to the chariots of day and night in the Edda or the chariot of the sun. The original chariot may have been built in the Aryan land … chariots are repeatedly mentioned in the "Vedas" as vehicles used by men on earth and gods above. These west country chariots are surely Aryan chariots.

170. In Swedish three princesses twist three threads with his hair. In Norse a princess throws three magnificent garments over the hero, which hewears under his own rough dress. All Gaelic versions agree in some mark, and nearly all in making it a mark on the head which the lady combs or otherwise arranges on the shore. The Swedish story of the "Three Swords" ends here. The Norse story of "Shortshanks" goes on with adventures to find a wife for a second brother. Other Swedish stories carry the tale further, and correspond with the Gaelic versions in a very remarkable manner.

176. Some reciters omit this part altogether. But it is part of the story and in other versions it is made a good deal of.... It is neither in Norse nor in Swedish.

The story of Jonah and the Whale may have suggested this, but if so it was suggested to Italians long ago. In "Straparola" the hero of the tale goes to the Atlantic ocean; a mermaid (*sirena*) begins to sing, he sleeps, and she swallows him. In like manner the mermaids sang that they might eat men, in the story of Ulysses. The oldest form of the similar myth is referred to in a note on No. 4. But that Varuna was a male divinity. This might be Varuna come to claim his promised victim.

187. This is chiefly from the telling of an old man in North Uist and of an old wife in Berneray. In "Straparola" the wife follows the husband to the Atlantic, in a ship, with her child, which was some years old. She gave the baby apples to play with on the deck; and for these apples the mermaid shows first the head, then the body to the waist, then the man to the knees, out of her mouth. He becomes an eagle, flies to the ship, and they all sail home. As the wife is taken, this tradition is more complete than it is in the old Italian or in any other version known to me. In the French version (*Cabinet des Fees*, tome 5, p. 49, 1785) the apples are turned into balls of gold and jewels. One is set with flat diamonds on all sides, the other is a large round emerald, the third is a ruby, and all three give out harmonies the most exquisite, which attracted the mermaid.

If I were not afflicted by honesty of purpose, it seems to me that the music, the object of price, and the dresses which were to ransom the husband might be combined and made to accord exactly with the rest of this story, by making the lady play upon the three whistles which the lad took from the giants, and which carried with them castles of copper, silver, and gold; with all the people and property stowed therein. That would be a good ransom and appropriate, but no Highland narrator has thus put the story together for me, and no book story that I know has either. I stick to truth in telling lies, and tell the tale as it is told in Gaelic.

188-206. ...not in Swedish, nor in Norse, nor in French, nor in Italian ... this mysterious egg nearly related to the egg of the Universe in Hindu, Greek, and Finnish myth.

207. The story now goes off to a second brother. In Swedish the second hero has adventures which are in German, but which I have not found in any Gaelic story. In Norse some of the adventures here given to a second brother are told of a widow's son separately. In Italian some of these adventures occur.

This second way is taken from versions in which a leash of creatures and adventures which they indicate, lead to fortune by courage, courting, and concealment, just as these creatures and many adventures led to fortune by courage and brute force, by swiftness and by cunning on the first road. The change made by me is simply to combine and to attribute adventures to a different brother in one case, to a different person in the other. The creatures met on this road are—(1) *Lion, Falcon, Rat*, in "The Second Son of the King of Ireland," got from Dewar and MacNair in Cowal, June 1860 (MS. No. 175); (2) *Lion, Dove, Rat*, in the "The Three Ways," got from MacLean and Margaret Mackenzie in Berneray, Harris, about same time (MS. No. 120). In this case the dove is the most appropriate bird, except where he has to carry warlike paraphernalia.

208. This natural history is all right. The rat meant is the little old Scotch rat now nearly banished by the so-called Hanoverian rat, but still to be found in the islands occasionally. He is a little short-tailed black creature, and I believe that he hibernates like a marmot.

210, 211. Bhima took service as cook, and Draupadi took service in the women's apartments, where her husband could not visit her.

228. This is the way the tale is told by a Highland shoemaker nowadays.

In "Straparola" an Italian princess gave Fortunio, who flew to her room as an eagle and hid in her slipper as an ant, arms and armour to go to a tournament where he overcame a Moor and a Turk. In Norway a princess gave the widow's son, who was the gardener's lad and her gallant, nothing, but he had a horse and harness. All these people tell this part of the story much in the same way, but each age and class and individual dresses the actors differently, and the Highlander gives the gallant an embroidered waistcoat to go to the fair.

240. In the "Mahabharata" a great man falls in love with the wife of the Pandavas; she gives him rendezvous, and Bhima meets him and slays him in the music and dancing room.

254. It does not appear how a pigeon carried armour, but that is not the fault of the translator.

275. According to Dewar, he was a second son of a king of Erin. The Irish king first married the daughter of the King of Scotland, and then after her death the daughter of the King of France. The stepmother tried to poison the boys, and they fled to seek their fortune. One went through these adventures and thus married his French cousin; the other went to serve with a farmer, and had no adventures in particular but married the farmer's daughter and reigned over Ireland after his father's death. The youngest brother went home, found his father sick, pretended to be a doctor, fetched his brother, consoled his father, and made him well. After that the stepmother was sent back to France, the stepson returned also to his bride, and all was made correct, accurate, and historical. The Berneray version is very short, but so far it agrees almost exactly with the Cowal version here condensed. It ends here with the wedding. This clearly is the story of one of three poor brothers who have Norse relations in "Shortshanks" and the "Widow's Son," and many other foreign relations of ancient lineage of whom the eldest are the five Pandavas in the "Mahabharata." (See *History of India*, by Talboys Wheeler, 1867.) The five Pandavas and their joint wife disguised themselves and served Raja Vivata for a year. They hid their arms in a tree on which they hung a dead body. Bhima the strong man and great eater became cook. From time to time he sallies forth, performed some feat and returned to the kitchen. At last with the brothers, of whom one was a herd and another a stableman, the cook rescued the king and defeated an army which had carried off the cows and the king. A fourth brother, Arunja, as a eunuch in female attire, taught singing and dancing in the palace till it was time to act. Then he became charioteer for the king's son, went to the tree, took his arms

and conquered another army which had captured more cows. The Raja claimed the victories for himself and for his son, and played at dice with the fifth brother, and insulted him. Then the five heroes revealed themselves and were greatly honoured. There can be no question about the identity of this very ancient Hindu legend with this part of this Gaelic story, and with the "Widow's Son" (*Norse Tales*, 364, etc.). There can be no question of borrowing from books in this case. Very few educated people know the name of the Indian epic.

The third set of adventures are in a tale of 89 manuscript Gaelic pages written by John Dewar, labourer, about the end of 1860. The tale was told to him by MacNair, shoemaker, at Clachaig in Cowal, near Dunoon, and he learned it about 1830 from MacArthur, a Cowal herring-fisher, who was an old "man of war's man." He was taken in the war and was in a French prison for a long time. I have sifted out parallel incidents such as the meeting with three enchanted creatures, the defence of the castle, the transformations and the conquest of a being whose life is in a mythical egg, from the old sailor's geographical sea-yarns so as to shorten and condense a very long precise and somewhat prosy story. (The MS. is bound in vol. viii.) A ship sails from Dublin to the East Indies: she goes to the Cape of Good Hope, and there, somewhere just beyond the limit of knowledge, the ship was lost. One sailor was saved, he found a path, went to a town, and found that he was in the Green Island where no ships called. He took service with the king's fisher, whose son had gone to school, though he was nearly twenty. The wife grumbled, for there was little fish to be had. One day they saw a ship (which is the mermaid transformed by the old sailor, of course). The whole sea-business of shortening sail and anchoring is described, the fisher goes on board, the sailor offers himself as a hand. The captain, in the mermaid's part, asks the fisher what family he has, and how he lives, and then the whole story is told over again to the captain, who says: "If you will bring me to-morrow here the first creature that meets you on shore, I will bring you plenty of fish." The sailor thought that his one-eared dog would be sure to meet him, so here is the dog (*cf.* the first part of the story). Then comes a long description of hand-line fishing, made mythical, and they loaded their boat with fish while the ship made sail, partly in technical sailor's language, partly in regular west country story-telling rhythm.

The fisher's son was the first creature met. The fisher had three daughters (who are characters in a Swedish version, but strangers here), and with the sailor they went to town, and sold the fisher's share of the fish. The fisher was sorrowful and his wife asked the cause, so he tells the whole story for the third time to his wife. The wife's counsel is to send the son to sea, so he was sent, but she laid it as crosses and spells on him to come back in a year and a day. The whole boat-sailing and ship-anchoring is repeated, and the new hand goes on board as the old sailor most probably did when he was young. They would not have the sailor, but they cast gold dust through the ports till the boat was nearly swamped, and they took the fisher's son and sailed away. The fisher got back and set the king's goldsmith to make coins, and then he was richer than the king. He gave his boat to the sailor, who fished for himself. The son sailed he knew not whither. One day they neared land, and he was sent on shore for water. He saw beautiful rare fruits, and he wandered from tree to tree plucking them; so here comes in the tree and forest myth which also belongs to this story. When he came back, boat, barrel, and ship had disappeared. Then he went up through the forest.

This is the first part of the myth. I have given this abstract to show how a story alters to suit the daily life and the experience of the narrator and his audience, and how easy it is to know incidents after learning the nature of oral mythology at the fountain-head amongst the people.

277. *Bha an latha falbh s bha an oidhche tighinn.* Such phrases are vernacular Gaelic, and are used without any thought of mythology. This, according to theory, is an ancient myth founded upon metaphorical Sanskrit phrases, used of speaking of day and night, sun and dawn. It may be, but in fact such phrases do not lead to personifications by those who now use them. In the next few pages are several more phrases literally translated to show the metaphorical nature of vernacular Gaelic used by peasantry without any double meaning at all. The peasant tells his story, another class of mind might easily join language and story, but the story itself comes first.

284. According to theory, here is a personification of light in her castle during the night. As the Gaelic for sun is feminine, here she is; but nobody in the West so understands the story. In Russian a similar passage is called the "Sun's Sister." I do but tell my tale and wait for more light, for I cannot

yet see my way to any theory which will account for my facts. In the "Edda" a female sun has a daughter who succeeds her mother after the twilight of the gods. In Japanese myth the sun is a lady who also is a snake divinity.

286. To me it seems that a moral lesson was intended by somebody. The first brother went headlong to his ends like a wolf, the second went swiftly and secretly like a bird, this one goes cautiously but courageously on. He does not go in till he has gone all round, he does not eat ravenously like a savage, but he waits patiently and politely as men do in the West; he eats frugally and he goes fearlessly on with his adventures. He is the youngest, and the youngest saves the others at the end of the story. The proverb "Slow and sure wins the race "—expresses the spirit of this class of story.

292. If he slept in the chamber of the dawn, of course not. But there is much to explain before any theory can be accepted. Here are six doors and a wall, which makes seven. In the story of Conall the castle had seven defences. The city of Ekbatana in "Herodotus" had seven walls; the city in the "Ramayana" had seven walls. The world, according to Hindu myth, consists of seven rings of land with seas between and a wall of mountains outside, beyond which is darkness. It would be the exploit of a divinity to pass seven such barriers and get to the mountain in the centre where the gods abide.

302. Any one who knows popular tales will here recognise Beauty and the Beast, Cupid and Psyche, Green Serpent, and a host of Western tales which are all allied to the Sanskirt story of Urvaçi. Theorists explain these by the ancient use of poor metaphorical language resulting in personification. Here is metaphorical language used by a labouring man without any double meaning whatsoever. When he says *the night came* he does not personify night. He speaks Gaelic and cannot avoid metaphor, but nevertheless he tells his mythical story which is all over the world in various forms and seems to be a lesson.

309. Here is a blank in the first part of the story. The first or second son, or both, ought to have gone home to enrich the old fisher after the mermaid's death, and the victory over the Turks.

316. The Gandharvas, who wanted Urvashi to return to them, caused her to look upon her husband by sending a flash of lightning after he had been enticed to rise from his couch. Here the case is reversed. The man sees the woman.

322. So far the story is that of Cupid and Psyche with the male character played by the actress. The recovery of the lost lady differs from any version known to me in any language.

328. Ants commonly live in skulls which bleach on the shore in the West Highlands. In fact, eagles do prefer to tear entrails.

329. The inferior personage who loses the superior in this widespread myth always needs some locomotive aid to arrive at the other place. Psyche has much to endure before she gets to Cupid in heaven. The Norse lassie who married the white bear got help from three old women who lent her three mythical horses, and then she flew upon the backs of four winged winds to the castle that was east of the sun and west of the moon. The Scotch lassies who married the black and red bulls of Norway got mystic fruits and gifts from three old wives, and iron shoes from a smith with which to cross a glass mountain. In No. 8 of the Swedish collection the lady is an "airmaid," and therefore is allied to a character Ilmaten in the "Kalevala." She comes in the shape of a dove to earth, and is caught. The youngest brother of a leash loses his bride and recovers her by getting boots, a cloak, and a sword from three brace of giants, and help from three old wives who ruled over beasts, and fish, and birds. It was "bird Fenix" who carried him to the castle that was east of the sun and north of the earth at last. In German, and in versions quoted from eight different languages in the Swedish collections, the myth, however, transformed has this common principle. The lost personage went skywards and had to be followed with wings. The question to be solved first is which form of the myth is nearest to the oldest shape of it. In Gaelic all this machinery exists, but in this tale it is all condensed into simple transformations, the gifts of beasts and birds and insects. Surely this is the simplest form and is most like an ancient religion. If the hero is one, the less help he needs the greater he is. These three brothers do not need to borrow horses, for horses were born with them. They do not need swords, for they grew with them. They do not need the locomotive boots or the cloak, or the

help of the old women who rule over beasts, or of the winds, because birds give them shapes and wings and swiftness; lions and wolves, courage and power. These three Atlantic fisher's sons are men with something of the sea in their nature, and with the nature of wild creatures added. They are superhuman in the story, and they surely were savage demigods once upon a time. In the oldest known form of the myth, the woman was an airmaid who came from the sky to marry a mortal. When Urvashi went away the mortal followed till he got leave to be one of the heavenly people called Gandharvas. This clearly is the story of Pururavas, but the puzzle is how it got to the West in this form. *Die Herabkunft des Feuers*, by A. Kuhn (Berlin, 1859, p. 31) contains the swan maiden story of Urvaçi. Part of the story is current in the Isle of Skye, and is in Grimm's "Three Eyes"; part of it is in New Zealand, Celebes, and Japan.

340. According to other versions of this incident, the lady ought to have wheedled this knowledge out of the giant at the instigation of her mortal lover (*v. Young King of Easaidh Ruadh* in Gaelic, the giant that had no heart in his body (Norse), and many German versions of this story). One modern theory would make the lady the dawn, or Ushas of the "Vedas"; the giant, winter or night or darkness; the egg, the sun; and the fisher's son, Indra or some other Vedic personification. Indra slew his foes by throwing one wheel of the sun's chariot at them in one battle. But Indra himself is exceedingly like a deified ancestor in the "Vedas." The myth seems rather to turn upon the mundane egg out of which everything was hatched; and some pantheistic notion of a common life for all things. If the aborigines held some such creed the conqueror may represent the creed of those who invaded them.

352. ... The reference to the sun may be taken as evidence in favour of those who count this an Aryan solar myth. The conversation of the lions tells for the water-myth theory, which I think most probable.

356. There is something of the story of David (Sam. i. 17, 33) and of Samson about this version which may have come into traditions out of the Bible. The other versions have no resemblance to holy writ.

400. J. F. C. here has a note on Swedish story and fire in a forest, and concludes that the story is not the property of any nationality, but is universal, human.

404. The incident of two people so like that they could not be distinguished by the wife of one occurs in the "Rigveda Sanhita" (*v.* Wilson's trans., vol. iii., 147-8). Indra was like a terrible lion when wielding his weapons, in which he resembles these fisher's sons in the Hebrides. The hymn says, "With a mind resolved on killing the Dasyu thou tamest to his dwelling, and Kutsa was eager for thy friendship. Now have you two alighted at Indra's dwelling, and being entirely similar in form the truthful woman has been perplexed to discriminate between you."

After a great battle in which Indra threw the wheel of the chariot of the sun and slew 50,000 black Rakshasas and other enemies, Indra took Kutsa home in his chariot to his palace where Sachi, Indra's wife, could not tell which of them was her husband.

In the story of Nala, given by T. Wheeler in his *History of India*, the lady who is to choose a husband sees five Nalas, for four gods have fallen in love with her and have taken the shape of her lover Nala. At her earnest prayers they leave her to her human lover, and endow him with mystical gifts.

NA TRÌ RATHAIDEAN MÓRA[90]

Bha duine bochd ann roimhe so agus bha trì gillean aige. Smaointich iad gum[91] fàgadh iad an athair agus gum falbhadh iad a dh'iarraidh an fhortain. Dh'fhalbh an triùir comhla air an aon rathad mhór. Bha iad a' falbh gos an d'thainig iad gu rathad mór a bha sgaoileadh 'na thrì miaran. Thuirt iad ri cheile an uair a chunnaic iad na trì rathaidean móra gon gabhadh gach fear aca rathad rathad mór air leth.

Ghabh am fear a bu[92] shine an rathad a bha dol an ear, 's ghabh am fear miadhonach an rathad a bha dol an iar, agus ghabh am fear òg an rathad miadhon. Air dha'n fhear a b'òige 'bhith treis air falbh choinnich leomhann is calman is radan e, 's iad a' sabaid. Thuirt an leomhann, "De, 'ghille, am beachd a th'agad orm fhìn a bhith 'na leithid so do dh'àite?" "Mata," ars' esan, "chan eil beachd agam ach nach ann an sin a bu chòir d' ur leithid a bhith, ach feadh bhruach aibhnichean." Chord so ris an leomhann agus thuirt e ris, "Na bi ann an càs a choidhch nach cuimhnich thu ormsa." Thuirt an radan ris: "De'm beachd a th'agad orm-sa 'bhith 'na leithid so do dh'àite?" "Chan eil beachd agam fhìn," ars' esan, "ach gor h-ann a bu choir duit a bhith a' cruinneachadh còs[93] an los e 'bhith agad a' feitheamh air a' gheamhradh." Chòrd so ris an radan agus thuirt e ris, "Na bi ann an càs a choidhch nach cuimhnich thu orm-sa."

---

[90] From Margaret Mackinnon, Berneray, who learnt it from John Morrison, Rusgary, Berneray, now a tenant in North Uist. August, 1859.

[91] eud gom. The pronoun 3rd pl. is eud, ead throughout.

[92] MS. bo.

[93] Porous material for fire.

Dh'fhoighneac an calman deth: "De 'bharail a th'agad orm fhìn a bhith anns an àite so?" "'S e a bharail a th'agam fhìn gor h-ann a bu chòir duit a bhith feadh gheugan is bhruthaichean is chreag," ars' esan. Chòrd so ris a' chalman 's thuirt e ris: "Na bi ann an càs a choidhch nach cuimhnich thu orm-sa."

Dh'fhalbh e, 's bha e a' falbh gun[94] tamh gun fhois gu[95] bial na h-oidhche; 's am bial na h-oidhche choinnich caisteal mór ris. Chaidh e stigh do'n chaisteal. Cha robh duin' a stigh 'sa chidsin an sin ach aona chòcaire—seana chòcaire mór—agus 's e'n còcaire mór a' theireadh iad ris.

Rinn e fasdadh; agus 's e'n obair a fhuair e bhith còcaireachd fo'n chòcaire mhór; agus s e'n còcaire beag a theireadh iad ris. Bha e dà oidhch' anns an tigh 's cha robh e 'faicinn bean idir. Dh'fhoighneac e ca'n robh h-uile bean a bha san tigh ud, an robh bean idir ann. "Chan eil ann ach nighean an righ, s chan e h-uile h-aon a gheibh thun a leapa," ars' an còcaire mór. Dh'fhoighneac e co'n àird de'n tigh an robh an seombar 's an robh i a' cadal. "Anns an àirde tuath," ars an còcaire.

Smaointich e air a chalman, 's chaidh e 'na chalman 's ghrad leum e gu mullach an t-simlear. An uair a ràinig e mullach an t-similear smaointich e air an radan 's chaidh e 'na radan 's ghrad leum e sìos gu bonn an àite-theine. Smaointich e'n sin air a bhith 'na dhuine 's chaidh e 'na dhuine 's dh'- fhalbh e thun leaba nighean an rìgh.

Thòisich e air cleasachd rithe, 's air an fhàinne bh' air a làimh a thoirt di. Lig' is' eubh. Thàinig a h-athair a nuas s bha esan 'na radan fo'n leaba. Thòisich a h-athair ri coinneamh a thoirt di airson a bhith 'g eubhach 's gun duin' anns an rum 'san robh i.

Cha bu luaithe dh'fhalbh a h-athair na chaidh esan 'na dhuin' a rithisd, 's a chaidh e chleasachd ris an fhàinne gus an d'thug e dhi e.

An uair a thug e dhi am fàinne smaointich e air an radan 's chaidh e 'na radan a suas gu barr an t-simlear. An uair a ràinig e bàrr an t-simlear

---

[94] Gon

[95] go.

168

smaointich e air a chalman 's chaidh e 'na chalman. Gheàrr e ite, 's chaidh e far an robh an còcaire mór 'sa chidsin.

De bha ach blàr mór ri bhith an la'r na mhàireach aig an righ ri righ cumhachdach eile. Nam biodh am blàr air a chur air an righ chailleadh e'n rìgheachd agus a nighean. Duine sam bith a chuideachadh leis gus am blàr a chur leis gheibheadh e a nighean ri 'phòsadh.

An la'r na mhàireach chruinnich a h-uile duine 's an rìgheachd a chur a chath leis an righ. Thug an còcaire beag an còcaire mór leis comhla ris.

An uair a bha'n righ treis a' cur a bhlàir de rinn e ach a chuimhneachadh gun d'fhàg e'n deise chruadhach a b'fhearr a bh' aige crochte ri taobh na leapa.

Dh' iarr e fear sam bith a bu luaithe a bheireadh 'a ionnsuidh an deise, e a' toirt 'a ionnsuidh chionn gun robh e smaointeachadh nam biodh i aige gun rachadh am blàr leis.

De 'rinn na gillean ach falbh 's a h-uile h-aon riamh dhiubh ruisgte gun traoidht[96] umpa. Dh'fhalbh an còcaire beag 'na chalman 's ràinig e'n tigh rompa 's dh'innis e do nighean an rìgh mar a bha 'm blàr a' dol. Thug e leis an deise chruadhach. An uair a bha àdsan[97] gos a bhith dhachaidh, de bha esan ach an deise chruadhach leis.

Thug e'n deise chruadhach thun an righ; agus de bha'm blàr ach a' dol air an rìgh an uair sin. Smaointich e air an leòmhann 's chaidh e 'na leòmhann; 's de a rinn e ach a h-uile gin de naimhdean an rìgh a thilleadh; 's reub is smùid is mharbh e a h-uile h-aon diubh 's chuir e'm blàr leis an rìgh.

An uair a chaidh am blàr leis an righ de 'bha ach an còcaire mór a' ràdh gur[98] h-e fhìn[99] a chuir am blàr. De bha'n oidhche sin ach reite gu bhith aig

---

[96] Probably a corruption of "thread," says Hector Maclean. Other variants are, *trìd, trait, tròidht*.

[97] For *iad-san*.

[98] Gor

[99] Dialectal.

nighean an righ 's aig a chòcaire mhór. Chruinnich a h-uile duine 's an rìgheachd[100] thun na reite.

Mu'n do thòisich an reite de dh' iarr an righ orr' ach dol a dhianamh[101] chleasan.

"Gad a theannainn fhìn ri dol a dhianamh chleasan chan eil fhios 'am[102] nach gabhadh sibh eagal," ars an còcaire beag.

Bha làn an tighe stighe de mhnathan uaisle 's de dhaoin uaisle aig an reite.

Dh'fhalbh e'n uair sin agus de a smaointich e ach a bhith 'na radan, 's chaidh e 'na radan. ... Smaointich e sin air a bhith 'na chalman 's chaidh e 'na chalman; is thòisich e le bun a sgeith ris an t-solusd 's ri bhith cur as an t-soluisd. Thòisich na mnathan uaisle ri ceol 's ri spòrs a ghabhail daibh fhìn[103] an uair a chunnaic iad duin' a' dol 'na chalman 's 'na radan. Chaidh esan an sin 'na leòmhann feadh an tighe, a' fosgladh a bhial airson a h-uile duin' itheadh; 's ma bha spòrs is ceòl aig na mnathan uaisle roimhid bha iad a nis air an oillteachadh a' teicheadh anns na cùilltean; 's cha b'e 'n còcaire mór a bu lugha ghabh do dh'oillt.

"Is fhior sin, 's cha bhrìagan," ars 'an rìgh; is tus', a ghille mhath, a chuir am blàr leom-sa, 's chan e 'm fear a tha 'dol a dh'fhaotainn mo nighinn r'a pòsadh."

Ghabh an còcaire mór a mach as an t-seombar leis an nàire, 's a h-uile duin' a' fochaid air; is phòs an còcaire beag agus nighean an rìgh.

---

[100] MS. rìghreachd.

[101] MS. has dhianadh.

[102] Short for *agam*.

[103] Dialectal.

AN T-IASGAIR[104]

Bha iasgair ann roimhid de sheann duine 's bhiodh e a' falbh a dh'iasgach daonnan. Latha dhe na làithean chaidh e dh'iasgach, 's cha robh e a' faighinn dearg. Am bial na h-oidhche de thachair ris ach iasg. Tharruinn e e, 's chuir e a làmh a mach a bhreith air. "An ann a brath mis' a thoirt leat a tha thu?" ars an t-iasg. "Matà 's ann, 's math leam gon d'fhuair mi thu," ars[105] an t-iasgair. "Chan e sin is fheàrra dhuit," ars an t-iasg, "ach lig mis' air m'ais 's theid thu g'a leithid so de dh'àite 'màireach 's gheibh thu go leòir de dh'iasg," ars an t-iasg. Lig e air ais e. Chaidh e dhachaidh. "An d'fhuair thu dearg idir?" ars a' bhean ris nur a chaidh e dhachaidh. "Cha d'fhuair," ars' esan, "gheibh mi gu leòir am màireach."

"Nach bochd a thàinig thu falamh an nochd," ars ise.

"Chan eil comas againn air," ars' esan.

An la'r na mhàireach dh'fhalbh e. Thug e fad an latha a' fiachainn am faigheadh e iasg, 's cha d'fhuair e dearg. Am bial na h-oidhche, an am tighinn dachaidh, rib an t-iasg e. Tharruing e'n t-iasg, 's rug e air go 'thoirt leis. "An ann a brath mo thoirt leat an nochd a tha thu?" ars an t-iasg. "'S ann," ars esan. "'S math leam t'fhaotainn gu d'thoirt leam." "Chan e sin is fheàrra duit, ach fàg mis' an nochd fhathasd, 's am màireach gheibh thu iasg na leòir." Dh'fhàg e e 's chaidh e dachaidh.

---

[104] 1 Reciter: Alasdair Mac Neill, Ceanntangaval, Barra; Alasdair Mac Ruairidh Bhàin. A very complete version with several new incidents not in printed version of the Mermaid.

[105] MS. urs.

"An d'thainig thu falamh an nochd a rithisd?" ars a' bhean. "Thàinig," ars esan. "O cha bhidh sinn beò," ars' ise. Chaidh e laighe 's chaidil e'n oidhche sin.

An la'r na mhàireach dh'fhalbh e dh'iasgach a rithisd 's cha robh e a' faighinn dearg. Am bial na h-oidhche nur a bha e 'dol dachaidh rib an t-iasg a rithisd e. Tharruinn e e 's rug e air. "An ann a brath mo thoirt leat a nochd a tha thu?" ars an t-iasg. "Matà 's ann," ars esan. "Chan fhàg thu' tuillidh mi?" "Chan fhàg," ars esan. "Chan eil duin' cloinn' agad?" ars an t-iasg. "Chan eil," ars esan. "Nur theid thu dhachaidh leam[106]-sa cha lig thu duine sam bith 'am sgoltadh ach thu fhìn.[107] Tha làir agad?" "Tha," ars am bodach. "Cha chuir thu anns a phoit an nochd ach bìdeag de'n ghrùthan 's bìdeag de'n chridhe dhuit fhìn, s do d' bhean 's do'n làir 's do'n ghalla. Gheibh thu'n sin trì chnàmhan aig taobh a chinn agam-sa agus theid thu mach agus tiodhl'caidh thu 'sa ghàradh iad. An oidhche bhios clann aig do bhean theid thu mach agus togaidh tu cnaimh agus cinnidh craobh far am bi'n cnàimh. Bidh trì mic aig do mhnaoi agus bidh trì craobhan an àite nan trì chnamhan a bhios fo shnodhach a shamhradh 's a gheamhradh a h-uile latha go bràch an eadh 's a bhios do chlann beò. H-uile siubhal a bhios mac aig do mhnaoi, bidh searrach aig an làir agus cuilean aig a ghala."

Chaidh e dachaidh, 's sgoilt e'n t-iasg 's chuir e bìdeag anns a phoite dha fhìn agus d'a mhnaoi, do'n làir agus do'n ghala, de'n ghrùthan 's de'n chridhe. Chaidh e laigh is chaidil e an oidhche sin.

An ceann trì ràithean thainig saothair chloinne air a mhnaoi, 's rug i leanabh mic. "De sin, a dhuine, a tha'n so?" ars ise. "Tha leanabh mic," ars esan. "Bu[108] mhath sin nam biodh rud ann a gheibheadh e," ars ise. "Tha sin ann," ars esan. Thug e sùil uaidh. Bha searrach aig an làir: bha cuilean aig a ghalla: bha craobh anns a ghàradh aig h-aon de na cnamhan.

An ceann trì ràithean bha leanabh mic aice. "De tha'n sin? a dhuin" ars ise. "Thà leanabh mic," ars esan. "Bu mhath sin," ars ise, "nam biodh rud ann a gheibheadh e." "Tha sin ann," ars esan. Thug e sùil uaidh 's chunnaic e'n

---

[106] MS. leom-sa.

[107] So MS.

[108] MS. bo.

darna searrach aig an làir 's an darna cù aig a ghalla 's an darna craobh as an darna cnàimh anns a ghàradh.

An ceann trì ràithean a rithist bha ### treas leanabh mic aice. "De tha'n sin, a dhuine?" ars ise. "Tha leanabh mic," ars esan. "Bu mhath sin nam biodh rud ann a gheibheadh e," ars ise. "Tha sin ann," ars esan. Thug e sùil uaidh 's chunnaic e'n treas searrach aig an làir 's an treas cù aig a ghala 's an treas craobh aig an treas cnàimh anns a ghàradh. Ghleidh am bodach na trì chnàmhan.

Bha a' chlann a' cinntinn suas gus an robh iad a' tighinn gu crìonnachd s gu gliocas. Thuirt am fear a bu shine r'a athair: bidh mi fhìn a'falbh a dh'iarraidh an fhortain. Chan eil sin ach bochd dhomh-sa an d'eis fhad 's a bha mi gun[109] 'ur faicinn," ars esan. Ma tha thu dol gu falbh tha each agus cù agad an so a rugadh an oidhche rugadh tu fhìn, 's bheir thu leat iad," ars am bodach. "Bheir thu leat strian agus thig an t-each 's cuiridh e 'cheann 'san strein." Thug e leis an strian 's chuir an t-each a cheann innte 's lean an cù e. Fhuair am bodach an cnàimh a bh'aig a chraoibh a chinn an oidhch' a rugadh e. Shìn e 'na laimh e 's dh'fhàs e 'na chlaidheamh chinn-òir 'na dhòrn.

"Taing duit, a rìgh nan ceud agus nan cumhachd," ars' an gille, "tha sgoil agus foghlum agus ionnsachadh agam-sa 'nis; ach a' chraobh ud 'sa ghàradh bidh i fo shnodhach 's fo dhuilleach bho fhoghar gu samhradh 's bho earrach gu geamhradh gus am faigh mis' am bàs 's nur a gheibh mis' am bàs tuitidh an snodhach di."

Dh'fhàg e beannachd aig athair 's aig a mhathair 's thug e gu astar. Gum bu cham gach rathad 's gum bu reidh gach slighe gus an d'rainig e pàileas righ na Gréige. Bha e gun chuid gun airgiod gun fios a bhi aige de a dhianadh e. Cha rachadh e stigh do'n phàileas. Ghabh e gus an tigh a b'iomallaiche bha'n sin uile gu leir ris an canadh iad tigh mucair. Cheangail e'n t-each aig an dorusd. Ghabh e stigh. Dh'fhoighnichd e'm faigheadh e

fantail an siud an nochd. Cha d'thuirt bean a mhucair am faigheadh no nach faigheadh. Cha robh duine cloinne aig a mhucair. Cha robh fios aige c'àit an

---

[109] MS. gon.

gabhadh e. Dh'fhan e far an robh e. Eadar sin agus treis dhe'n oidhche tighinn thainig am mucair. Dh'fhoighnichd e co bu leis an t-each a bh'aig an dorusd. Thuirt an t-òganach gum bu leis-san.

"A bhean, an d'thug thu biadh do'n choigreach?" ars am mucair. "Cha tug, cha d'iarr e orm e," ars ise. "Deasaich biadh dha." Thòisich i air deasachadh bidh dha. "De'n naigheachd a th'agad as a' bhaile mhór?" ars a bhean. Na bha naigheachdan agam-sa tha fios agad fhìn orra ach chan eil fhios 'am am bheil fios aig a choigreach air. Chan eil de mhic no nigheanan aig righ na Greig' ach an aon nighean. Thainig brath 'a ionnsuidh mur am bi e am màireach aig a' chladach le a aon nighean 'a toirt air dheas làimh do Mhaca Mór Rìgh na Sorcha, gur e a' chlach is àirde clach is ìsle, 's a' chlach is ìsle clach is àirde 'na chaisteal. Chruinnich e na bha 'na rioghachd de shluagh uile gu leir cuideachd, fiach am faigheadh e duine sam bith a dh'fhalbhadh a ghleidheadh na nighinn, 's gum faigheadh e'n darna leith d' a rioghachd ri 'bheò, 's an rioghachd uile gu leir air a mharbh, 's a nighean r'a phòsadh.

Cha d'fhuair e duine beò a ghabhadh as laimh falbh leis an nighinn ach aona chòcaire claghann ruadh a bha a' gearradh feòl' a stigh aige le sgithinn mhóir. Cuiribh an t-suipeir air dòigh," ars an t-òganach a thainig, 's biodh a bhraiceas reidh tràth, chionn tha rnis a' falbh tràth anns a' mhaduinn, 's gnothaichean agam ri urrachan móra. Thig mi rithisd 'san anmoch.

Dh'fhalbh e 'sa' mhaduinn. Ghabh e air muin an eich 's lean an cU e. Chunnaic e nighean rìgh na Gréige 's an cocaire claghann ruadh ri a taobh; sgian mhór aige 'na dhòrn an àite claidheamh. "Gad a thigeadh na bheil san t-Sorcha, siud mar a dhianainn-sa orra," theireadh an còcaire claghann ruadh, 's e 'dinneadh na sgithinn anns a ghainmhich. Ghobh[110] e null far an robh iad 's bheannaich e do nighean righ na Gréige 's bheannaich nighean righ na Gréige dha. "Obh! obh," ars an cocaire claghann ruadh, "de tha'n so, no de a thachair oirnn?" "Fiach am falaich thu mis'," ars esan. "De'm falach a ni mis' ort?" ars ise. Rug i air 's thilg i ann an àite dugharrach e far am faiceadh e h-uile duine 's nach faiceadh duin' e. "Nach falamh a thàinig thu'n so, a nighean rìgh na Gréige," ars an t-òganach. "Cha robh duine beò anns an rioghachd a thigeadh comhla rium ach còcaire claghann ruadh a bh'aig m'athair."

---

[110] = ghabh.

"Suidhidh mi fhin comhla riut treis," ars esan. "De's ciall-dùsgaidh dhuit ma thig an cadal ort?" ars ise. "Mo chuilean gaolach fhìn mo tharruinn leis an rann s mo tharruing an aghaidh an ranna." Ann an ùine ghoirid thuit esan na chadal. Cha b'fhad a bha e 'na chadal nur a chunnaic is' an fhiarge a' dol dha'n iar 's am muir a' fàs mór.

"A chuilean ghaolaich," ars' ise, "dùisg do mhaighstir."

Dh'fhalbh an cuilean agus tharruing e leis an rann e agus an aghaidh an ranna 's dhùisg e e. Nur a sheall e uaidh chunnaic e òlach moidearra misgiamhach a' tighinn ann an luing. Dhianadh e stiùir 'na deireadh 's ball 'na toiseach. Gach ball a bhiodh fuasgailte gun ceangladh e, 's gach ball a bhiodh ceangailte gum fuasgladh e. A' mhuc a bu mhotha ag itheadh na muice bu[111] lugha 's a' mhuc a bu lugha a' dianamh[112] mar a dh'fhaodadh i: faochaga croma ciar a' chladaich a sior urgadaich air a h-ùrlar aig fheobhas 's bha'n t-òigear 'ga stiùradh. Ghabh e gu àit acair leatha 's leag e a cuid sheòltan. Thug e'n dùgh-dheireadh aice 'ionnsuidh an dùgh-thoisich. Thug e leum an sin

air tìr 's tharruing e air tir air tràigh Thug e'n ath leum a stigh 'na broìnn 's thòisich e air e fhin[113] a chur 'na eideadh. Ghabh mac an Iasgair sios 's sheall e air a fad agus air a liad. Chuir e a dhà laimh timchioll oirre 's thog e i 's dh'fhàg e i 'sia fad fhìn am bràigh na tràgha i.

"Co'n aona bheadagan a bha'n rioghachd na Gréige aig an robh a chridhe a leithid siud de bhallachd-buird[114] a dhianamh orm fhìn no air mo luing? Ach bheir mise air righ na Gréige a gheall a bhith le a nighinn 'a toirt domh air dheis laimh air a chladach, gur h-i a' chlach is isle clach is àirde, 's a' chlach is àirde clach is isle 'na chaisteal, mur an cum e a ghealladh rium-sa," ars am fear a bha 'san luing. Tha e'n so fhathast 's cha do theich e 's chan eil duine 'n rioghachd na Gréige is miosa na mise," arsa mac an Iasgair. Thòisich an dithisd air a cheile. Dhianadh iad bogan air a'chreagan agus creagan air a'

---

[111] MS. bo.

[112] MS. dianadh.

[113] So MS.

[114] Mockery. Phrase: dh'fhàg e ballachd air = he left a mark on him.

bhogan; an t-àite bu lugha rachadh iad fodha rachadh iad fodha gu'n glitinean; 's an t-àite bu mhotha rachadh iad fodha rachadh iad fodha g'an sùilean. Smaointich mac an Iasgair gum bu dona dha tuiteam anns a' chiad bhlàr 's an d'fhiachadh e. Thug e'n togail ud air agus leag e e. "Am bàs as do chionn! de t'eirig?" arsa mac an Iasgair. "'S mór sin, 's mi mac mór righ na Sorcha. Ach de'm bàs a tha thu brath a thoirt domh?" ars esan. "De'm bàs a bheireadh tu fhìn domh-sa nam biodh tu an deigh mo leagail an toiseach?" arsa mac an Iasgair. "An ceann a thoirt as an amhuich agad," arsa mac mór righ na Sorcha. "Matà chan e sin a ni mis' ort-sa," ars esan, "ach cuiridh mi ceangal an taod gu daor agus gu docair ort, agus mionnan, gach buill' a bhuaileas thu gum buail thu le righ na Gréige e agus gum bi thu 'nad ghaisgeach dùrachdach dha gu bràch." Dh'fhalbh e 's thug e leis e suas gu bàrr a' bhruthaich, 's dh'fhàg e'n sin e. Ghabh e air muin an eich 's ghabh e dachaidh.[115]

Chaidh an còcaire claghann ruadh dhachaidh le nighean an rìgh mar gum b'e fhìn a dhianadh an treubhas. Chuireadh cairt agus gille a dh'iarraidh mhic mhóir righ na Sorcha. Chuireadh e fo shileadh na lòchraidh 's fo ròs choinnlean. Rainig mac an Iasgair tigh a mhucair. Chuireadh biadh is deoch air a bhial-thaobh. Cha b'fhad a bha e stigh nur a thainig am mucair dachaidh. Dh'fhoighnic mac an Iasgair de'n naigheachd a bh' aige. Thuirt e gur minic[116] a theireadh nach robh claidheamh math an droch thruaill aig a chòcaire chlaghann ruadh agus an t-euchd a rinn e. Ach tha e'm màireach ri falbh fhathasd agus an earar, ars am mucair. "Tubaist air na daoin-uaisle bha gnothuch agam fhìn riu 's cha d'fhuair mi aig an tigh iad 's feumaidh mi falbh am màireach fhathast."

Chaidh e laigh an oidhche sin 's chaidil e. Moch 's a mhaduinn dh'eirich e 's an deigh a bhiadh a ghabhail chaidh e air muin an eich 's dh'fhalbh e. Ghabh e lom, dìreach far an robh nighean rìgh na Gréige: chuir e a cheann air a glùn.

"De 's ciall-dùsgaidh dhuit ma thuiteas thu 'd chadal?" ars ise. "Thà, barr na lùghdaig' deis' a thoirt diom," ars esan. Ann an ùine ghoirid chaidil e. Cha

---

[115] Barra dialect.

[116] Barra dialect for mairg.

robh e fada 'na chadal nur a chunnaic is' an soitheach a' tighinn. Thug i dheth barr na lughdaig dheis 's dhuisg e.

Thainig mac miadhonach righ na Sorcha gu tìr. Choinnich mac an Iasgair e 's rinn e a' cheart leithid air 's a rinn e air a bhrathair an de. Chaidh e air muin an eich s ghabh e air falbh.

Chaidh an còcaire claghann ruadh dhachaidh le nighean an rìgh 's co ach esan 's e 'cumail a mach gur h-e fhìn a bha 'dianamh gach gniomh gaisgeil. An am an athaidh agus an anmoich ghabh mac an iasgair gu tigh a' mhucair mar a b'àbhaist. Cha b'fhad' a bha e stigh nur a thainig am mucair dachaidh. "'S minig[117] a theireadh nach robh claidheamh math an droch thruaill aig a chòcaire chlaghann ruadh," ars am mucair. "De an t-euchd a rinn an còcaire claghann ruadh an dràsd?" arsa mac an Iasgair. "Mac miadhonach righ na Sorcha a cheangal," ars' am mucair. "Tha'm màireach agam fhìn ri thoirt fhathast mar a bh'agam an diu," arsa mac an Iasgair.

An la'r na mhàireach chaidh e air muin an eich 's dh'fhalbh e. Rainig e far an robh nighean righ na Gréige. Chuir e a cheann air a "De's ciall-dùsgaidh dhuit ma chaidleas thu?" ars ise. "Barr na lughdaig eile a thoirt diom," ars esan. An ùine ghoirid thuit e 'na chadal. Cha b'fhad a bha e 'na chadal nur a chunnaic ise soitheach a' tighinn. Thug i barr na lughdaig eile dheth 's dhùisg e. Chaidh an còcaire claghann ruadh am falach leis an eagal mar a b'àbhaist da. Thainig mac beag righ na Sorcha air tìr. Rinn mac an Iasgair air mar a rinn e air càch. Chaidh e air muin an eich s ghabh e air falbh. Chaidh an còcaire claghann ruadh dhachaidh le nighean an rìgh, s co ach esan, 's mu b'fhior e fhìn gur h-e rinn gach euchd. Thugadh mac beag righ na Sorcha ceangailte gu tigh an righ, s bha nis' triuir mhac righ na Sorcha ceangailte stigh fo shileadh na lòchraidh 's fo ròs nan coinnlean[118]; s gach cnàimh a lomadh na h-uaislean aig a chuirm ga thilgeadh orra le masladh agus le tàmailte. Anns an fheasgair rainig mac an Iasgair tigh a mhucair. Cha robh e fad a stigh nur a thainig am mucair. "De do naigheachd an nochd?" arsa mac an Iasgair ris a' mhucair. "Tha sin agam naigheachd," ars' am mucair, "gum bheil triuir mhac righ na Sorcha a nis ceangailte aig a

---

[117] For mairg

[118] Beneath the drippings from the black (sooty) rafters and the resin of the (pine) candles.

chòcaire chlaghann ruadh 's gum bheil e fhìn agus nighean an righ ri pòsadh am màireach." "Nach e'n gaisgeach e," arsa mac an Iasgair.

Bha banais eibhinn shunndach aighearach ri bhith aig nighean an righ 's aig a' chòcaire ruadh. Chuireadh brath air a h- uile duine b'urrainn coiseachd anns an rioghachd thun na bainnse. Chuireadh b rath air a mhucair 's cha d'fhiathaicheadh an coigreach; 's cha rachadh am mucair ann o'n nach robh esan a' dol ann. "De bu choireach, a mhucair, nach deachaidh thu-sa thun na bainnse?"[119] ars' mac an Iasgair. "Cha rachainn-sa ann agus thu fhìn fhàgail," ars' am' mucair. "'S math am bord-bainnse th'aig nighean righ na Gréige an dràsd," arsa mac an Iasgair, "b'fhearr leam fhìn gun robh e againn air ar bial-thaobh. Fhalbh[120] thus, a chuilein ghaolaich, agus sìn thu fhìn agus na bi ceacharra a'dol suas. Theirig a steach do sheombàr na bainnse agus an tuthailt tha sìnte air a' bhord air bial-thaobh an rìgh agus bhean-nabainnse, thoir thugam-sa an so e."

Dh'fhalbh an cù agus ghabh e suas. Chaidh e stigh do'n t-seombar. Rug e air an tuthailt agus chruinnich e i 's thug e leis Ghabh e sios leatha gu tigh a mhucair. Sgaoil e air a bhord air am bial-thaobh i.

"Am bheil duine sam bith," ars comhairleach a bh'aig an righ, "nach eil an so fhathasd? 's fhad o'n a chuala mi e: 's làidir cui.lean a uchd treòir. Fhalbhaibh agus seallaibh am bheil am mucair a stigh, no co tha comhla ris."

Ghabh iad a sios 's chunnaic iad a h-uile sgath de na bh'air a bhòrd air bial-thaobh a' mhucair agus a' choigrich. "Thuirt mi roimhid: 's làidir cuilean a uchd treòir. 'S minic (i.e. mairg) a dhianadh a leithid siud de bhanais do'n chòcaire chlaghann ruadh, 's nach creid mi gur h-e a cheangail na gaisgich," arsa 'n comhairleach nur a thill an fheadhainn a chaidh sios 's a dh'innis iad mar a bha. "Falbhadh a' bheag-bhuidheann ghaisgeach sìos is thugadh iad a nios am ionnsuidh-sa ceangailt' e," ars an righ.

"Ghabh a bhuidheann sìos. Co dh'iarr oirbh-se na bh'air bòrd an righ thoirt leibh?" arsa na chaidh a sios ris a mhucair agus ri mac an Iasgair. "Cha d'thug sinne leinn riamh e, 's cha do chairich sinn as a so fhathast," arsa mac

---

[119] Was not invited.

[120] MS. Thalla.

178

an Iasgair. "Mur an d'thug thusa leat e thug do chù leis e agus tha do chù mìomhail," ars' àd-san. "Na bithibh a' bruidhinn ris ach beiribh air, 's thugaibh leibh ceangailte e, mar a dh'iarradh oirnn," arsa fear de'n bhuidheann."

"Eirich[121] thu-sa, 'chuilean, agus tarruinn iad leis an rann, agus tarruinn iad an aghaidh an ranna anns an lùb ud a muigh," arsa mac an Iasgair.

Rug an cuilean orra agus tharruing e iad an aghaidh an ranna agus leis an rann anns an lùba. Dh'fhalbh iad suas 'nan conablaich mar sin dh'ionnsuidh an righ.

"Nach d'thuirt mi roimhid gum bu làidir cuilean a uchd treòir," ars an comhairleach. "Fhalbh thus'," ars an righ r'a ghille agus cuir an òrdugh an *coach* agus gun rachamaid a dh'iarraidh a' choigrich." Chuir an gille an òrdugh an coach agus chaidh an righ agus a nighean a dh'iarraidh a' choigrich. Chan fhalbhadh e leo gun am mucair a bhith leis. Chaidh e fhin s am mucair an sin a stigh 'sa *choach* leis an righ agus le a nighean agus dh'fhalbh iad gu tigh an righ. Chaidh iad a stigh do sheombar na bainnse agus shuidh iad. "Tha rud a dhìth a nis orm-s," ars' nighean an rìgh, "agus suidhibh socair samhach timchioll an tseombair" 's ràinig i esan. "Cuir a mach do lamh," ars' ise. "Tha mo lamh goirt," ars esan. Thug i spadhadh air a laimh 's tharruinn i mach Chuir i'n sin a lamh 'na pòca, 's thug i barr na lughdaig deis' aig as 's chuir i siud air a lughdaig.

"'S fior sin," ars ise, "'s tu-sa rinn an t-euchd. Cha bhi dh'fhear pòsda no dìolain agam-sa gu brach ach thu-sa; 's cuiribh air a h-aghaidh a bhanais."

Dh'eirich esan 's chaidh e sios 's dh'fhuasgail e triùir chloinne righ na Sorcha. Thugadh dachaidh pears' eaglais is phòs iad. Chaidh iad a laighe is chaidil iad an oidhche sin. An là'r na mhàireach thug e sùil uaidh a null a mach air an uinneig 's chunnaic e caisteal dubh thall mu a choinneamh. Dh'fhoighnie e de 'n caisteal a bha'n siud. Thuirt ise ris nach robh ach caisteal a bh'aig an droch chreutair. Dh'eirich[122] e 's ghabh e mach. Thug e

---

[121] MS. (dialectal).

[122] MS. dh'éiridh

leis 'each agus a chù 's ghabh e null 'ionnsuidh a chaisteil. Chaidh e stigh 's chunnaic e boirionnach an sin 's i a' cireadh a cinn.

"Co as a thàinig thu, a mhic athar mo ghaoil agus mathar mo ghràidh? Thig a nios 's gun innseadh tu naigheachd domh 's gun innsinn-sa naigheachd duit." Ghabh e sìos far an robh i. Rug i air an t-slachdan dhraoidheachd 's rinn i carragh-creige dheth. Rinn i leithid eile air a chù agus air an each. Sheall am bodach am mach 's bha a' chraobh an deigh an duilleach a chall. "'S fior sin," ars' esan, "tha mise gun mhac an diu." "Tha mis' a' falbh," ars am mac miadhonach gus am faigh mi eirig mo bhrathar a thogail." Chaidh e air muin eich 's lean a chù e 's thug am bodach dha cnàimh 's dh'fhas an cnàmh 'na chlaidheamh chinn-òir 'na laimh. "Tha ionnsachadh is fòghlum agam-sa a nis," ars esan is dh'fhalbh e. Gum bu cham gach rathad 's gum bu reidh gach slighe gus an d'thainig e lom dìreach gu tigh a' mhucair. Cha do chruthaicheadh na bu choltaiche r'a cheile na e fhein is a bhrathair.

"De thug dhuit fuireachd an raoir o aobhar do mhnatha agus do leannain?" Chuireadh suas gu tigh an rìgh e. Ghabh ise 'na choinneamh agus 'na chomhdhail 's dùil aice gur h-e a fear a bh'ann. Cha robh fios aige air an t-saoghal de mar a gheibheadh e fantail gun dol a leaba 'bhrathar an oidhche sin. Se thuirt e rithe gun robh geall mór eadar e fhìn agus duin' uasal 's nach b'urrainn e dol a laighe, ach gun caidleadh e air a bhord aig bial na leapa. Rinn e siud. Thug e sùil uaidh anns a mhaduinn 's de chunnaic e ach an caisteal. "De'n caisteal a tha'n siud?" ars e rithe-sa. "Nach d'innis mi sin duit an oidhche roimhid?" ars ise. Dh'eirich[123] e 's chaidh e mach. Thug e leis 'each 's a chù 's ghabh e null 'ionnsuidh a chaisteil. Chaidh e stigh 's rinn is' air mar a rinn i air a bhrathair.

Sheall am bodach a mach 's bha'n duilleach air tuiteam bharr an darna craobh.[124] "'S fhior sin," ars am mac òg, "cha bheò mo bhrathair. Bidh mise a' falbh a thogail 'eirig."

Thug e leis 'each 's a chù. Thug 'athair cnàimh dha 'na laimh. Dh'fhàs an cnaimh 'na chlaidheamh chinn-òir 'na dhòrn.

---

[123] MS. dh'éiridh.

[124] Usually *craobh* is feminine.

"Taing dhuit-s', a righ nan ceud 's nan cumhachd: tha gach ionnsachadh is fòghlum agam-sa a nis."

Ghabh e air falbh. Gum bu[125] cham gach slighe 's gum bu reidh gach rathad da gus an d' ràinig e pàileas righ na Gréige. Chunnaic ise mach thromh na h-uinneagan e 's ghabh i mach 'na choinneamh agus 'na chomhdhail. Thug i leatha dhachaidh e. "Bha na leòir duit fuireachd a chiad oidhche gun fuireachd an raoir," ars ise, 's i a' saoilsinn gur h-e a fear a bh'ann.

"'S iomadh duine a bhios gnothuch aige ri uaislean air chor 's nach bi fios aca c'uin a thig iad," ars esan. Chaidh iad a laighe 's chuir esan claidheamh fuar eatorra. Anns a' mhaduinn an là'r na mhaireach thug esan sùil uaidh, 's chunnaic e caisteal mar a chunnaic càch. Dh'fhoighnic e de'n caisteal a bha'n siud. "Nach d'innis mi sin duit an raoir 's an oidhche roimh sin?" ars ise. Dh'eirich e 's thug e leis 'each 's a chù 's ghabh e null thun a chaisteil. Chaidh e stigh 's chunnaic e boirionnach an sin a' cìorradh a cinn.

"Thig a nios, 'fheudail, a mhic athar mo ghaoil agus màthar mo ghràidh,'s gun innseadh tu naigheachd domh, 's gun innsinn naigheachd duit," ars ise. Cha robh amharus math sam bith aig oirre.[126] Thug e'n leum sin a suas 's leag e i 's chuir e'n claidheamh air an amhuich aice.

"Am bàs as do chionn! De t'éirig?" ars esan. "Is mór sin," ars ise. "Drong òir agus drong airgid." "Is leam sin agus do bhàs," ars esan. Thug e'n ceann di. Thug e uaithe na h-iuchraichean 's dh'fhiach e'n tigh. Fhuair e aon seòmbar làn òir is airgid. Fhuair e seòmbar làn aodaichean dhaoin'uaisle. Fhuair e seòmbar làn dhìollaidean agus strianan. Fhuair e seòmbar làn bhrògan agus bhòtainnean. Fhuair e seòmbar làn dhaoin air an tionndadh 'nan carraghnan creige. Rug e air ballan an ath-bheothachaidh 's thòisich e air a dhòrtadh orra gus an d'thug e beò iad. Bha a bhràithrean fhìn 'nam miosg. Thug e 'aodach 's a chuid fhìn do na h-uile duine bha'n sin agus dòrlach òir is airgid. Chaidh e fhìn 's a bhràithrean a suas gus a' phàileas.

"Is ann agad," ars esan r'a bhràthair, "a tha'n aon bhoireannach is fhean air an do shil uisg' athar riamh.

---

125 MS. gom bo.

126 MS. urra.

"Dé mar tha thu-sa 'ga aithneachadh sin?" ars a bhràthair.

"Is ann comhla rithe bha mi fhìn an raoir," ars esan. Bhuail an t-eud a bhràthair agus tionndar ris agus tilgear an ceann deth leis a chlaidheamh.

Sheall am bodach a mach agus bha a' chraobh aig an fhear òg air tuiteam 's bha'n dà chraobh eile 'nan seasamh.

"Is fhior e," ars esan. "Tha mo mhac as òige marbh, 's tha'n dithisd eile beò 'rithisd."

Bha'n dà bhràthair an oidhche sin am pàileas an rìgh. An la'r na mhàireach dh'fhalbh iad 'nan dithisd ann an *coach*. Ràinig iad tigh an athar. Thug iad leò e, e-fhìn 's am mathair gu pàileas righ na Gréige. An la'r na mhàireach chuir iad iad an caisteal daibh fhìn. Bha'n rìoghachd aig a' bhràthair bu shine agus nighean an righ aige pòsda.

www.ingramcontent.com/pod-product-compliance
Lightning Source LLC
Chambersburg PA
CBHW020640180626
46816CB00003B/1052